Pearls of Childhood

Pearls of Childhood

VERA GISSING

St. Martin's Press
New York

My thanks to my friend Susie Saunders, for her enthusiastic encouragement and invaluable help, particularly with editing the completed manuscript.

Library of Congress Cataloging-in-Publication Data

Gissing, Vera.
      Pearls of childhood / Vera Gissing.
          p.   cm.
      ISBN 0-312-02963-2
       1. Gissing, Vera. 2. Jews—Great Britain—Biography.
  3. Refugees, Jewish—Great Britain—Biography. 4. Jewish children-
-Great Britain—Biography. I. Title.
DS135.E6G574   1989
941'.004924024—dc19
[B]   89-4130
                                                CIP

First published in Great Britain by Robson Books Ltd.

First U.S. Edition

10 9 8 7 6 5 4 3 2 1

In Memory of Mother and Father

Contents

Note on accents:

My beloved Czech language uses accents; my adopted English does not. As I thought a page spattered with unfamiliar marks might put off an English reader I omitted all accents in the text. However, for those who might be interested in what Czech looks and sounds like, I have given below a list of proper names and their pronunciation.

As in book		Czech form	Pronunciation
Vana, *the name of our horse*		Váňa	Vahnia
tatícek	} 'daddy'	tatíček	taticheck
tatínek		tatínek	tatteeneck
maminka	'mummy'	maminka	mamminka
maminko	} *the vocative case,*		
tatinku	} *used in direct address*		
Veruska	} *diminutive or pet*	Věruška	Vierushka
Evicka	} *forms of Věra and Eva*	Evička	Evichka
Celakovice, *our town*		Čelakovice	Chelahkovicer
Benes, *the President in exile*		Beneš	Benesh
na shledanou, 'au revoir'		Na shledanou	Nah skledanoe
nazdar, 'hello'		nazdar	nazdaar
Terezin, *a border town*		Terezín	Terredzeen
Dasa, *a girl's name*		Dáša	Dahsha
Zajicek, *a professor*		Zajíček	Zaheecheck
Marenka, *diminutive form of the name Marie*		Mařenka	Matrenka
Hradcany, *a castle*		Hradčany	Hradchanny
Mila, *a girl's name*		Míla	Meelah

Introduction

FORTY YEARS ON . . .

As the private coach wound its way out of London and headed towards Wales, I sat down in my seat with a sigh of contentment and relief. We were on our way at last and already the venture bore the mark of success.

The forty middle-aged passengers were talking away happily, without a trace of awkwardness, shyness or reserve. To any onlooker the scene would have appeared that of a large close-knit family, or of intimate friends. No one could have guessed that the last time we had all been together we had been no more than children, and that many had travelled great distances, some half-way across the globe, just to meet up again.

It was June 1985 – and this was the year for 'forty years on' reunions of those who had shared experiences of the Second World War. We too were on our way to such a gathering and expected to be joined by at least another thirty people at our destination, the Abernant Lake Hotel in Llanwrtyd Wells. The little Breconshire town, which in our childhood years was just a village, and the hotel both have a special place in our hearts, because the hotel was our wartime school and home, and Llanwrtyd Wells 'our' village which had opened its doors and hearts to us. There we had spent the most vital, the most impressionable and memorable years of our lives.

When we first arrived at the school we were a very mixed bunch of children, but we had one thing in common: we were all refugees who had fled to Britain from Nazi-occupied Czechoslovakia. Some had escaped with their parents, but many, like me, came on their own in children's transports. That we managed to get away was entirely due to the foresight, concern and efforts of various British religious organisations and individuals. In the uneasy months prior to the outbreak of war, when the British government was still hoping for peace, these organisations, greatly disturbed by what was happening in Europe, found homes and guarantors, and a rescue operation was set up which saved thousands of young lives from occupied territories.

It was not until March 1988 that I learned that the key figure in the life-saving mission of rescuing children from Czechoslovakia was Nicholas Winton, then a young stockbroker, who took on the task and responsibility to bring out as many as humanly possible. Convinced that war was imminent and that there was no time to lose, he opened an office in Prague three months before Hitler marched in, and compiled lists of children in danger. Back in England, he intensified the search for sponsors and foster-parents, handled all the complex paperwork connected with entry permits and visas and arranged the train transports. His incredible efforts resulted in 664 children escaping Hitler's clutches. I was one of them . . . Not all, but most, of us were Jewish, and had we remained in our own country we would have been bound not for Britain, but for a concentration camp and an almost certain death. We were the lucky ones, thanks mainly to Nicholas Winton. To him we owe our freedom and life . . .

Many of the transport children eventually joined the Czechoslovak school which was founded in 1940, after the fall of France. The school provided us with the unique opportunity to continue our education in exile in a Czech environment. Moreover, it gave us an anchor, a sense of belonging and security when we needed it most. It was our home, we were a family, and the closeness which grew out of adversity survived distance and time. In those days we shared not only our lives, but our fears and our dreams, which for many of us would be shattered.

When the war ended in the summer of 1945, the school closed and we all went our separate ways. Most of us were repatriated to Czechoslovakia, only to find that our parents and families had perished in the holocaust; some remained in Britain, some moved to other countries and continents. During the intervening years we met occasionally in small groups, and kept in touch with one or two school friends. But no attempt to organise a reunion on a grand scale had ever been made.

It was in the late summer of 1984 that four of us happened

10

to meet when Seppi, one of my Washington-based class-mates, was passing through London. Over dinner the idea of the reunion was born; by the time we were drinking coffee the date had been fixed and a plan was beginning to take shape. Before we parted we had decided that Honza, Harry and I, the three Londoners present, would tackle the task of putting the plan into operation.

We spent over a year tracking down the members of our old school by various means. As they had scattered throughout the world this was a considerable task, but eventually we managed to locate well over a hundred.

The response and reaction were overwhelming, and the numbers of those hoping to attend the reunion rose steadily. The replies confirmed that nearly everyone still looked upon the years we had shared with great nostalgia.

Now at last it was really happening. Drawn together by the echoes of our childhood years, we were on our way to spend the weekend in the very hotel in which our school had been housed. And already it seemed as if the forty intervening years had melted away.

As I sat there, recalling those unforgettable schooldays, other memories came flooding back, penetrating beyond that period of joy, uncertainty and grief, to the days of 1937 when life was still wonderfully carefree and I was a little girl leading an ordinary, happy life with my sister and my parents in a free Czechoslovakia.

I knew then that somehow I would find the strength to open and reread my diaries I had kept through the war, and my parents' letters which had been locked away for all the forty years and, through them, to relive the past. Suddenly I felt compelled to tell my story, which, to a great extent, is the story of all those who were torn away from their homes as children, and who found refuge, help and understanding here in Britain.

PART I

Pearls of Childhood

1

'My Little Girl is Growing up Fast'

ONE OF THE last vivid memories of my childhood is of the summer in 1937 when I was nine years old and for the very first time on holiday without my parents. The children's camp in which I was spending a month was situated in a beautiful sunny valley sliced in two by the fast-flowing river Sazava. The surrounding hills were thick with pine forests; their heady scent perfumed the air and their dark greenness was a stark contrast to the bright blue of the summer sky. Our dormitories were wooden huts on stilts, our dining room a meadow. We only ate under canvas when it rained. The large tent, big enough to seat all fifty of us, was used for almost everything when the weather was bad. The aim of the camp, which accepted children aged seven to twelve, was not only to give parents a break, but also to teach us to be independent and unafraid, even when spending a lonely night in a small tent at the edge of the forest. The days were packed with outdoor activities, the still warm evenings were spent singing and listening to stories round a huge camp-fire. As darkness fell and the moon and stars became the only visible focal points outside our small, close circle, I felt there was no other world outside our little fire-lit group under that vast sky.

I loved the camp but I was terribly homesick. I had never been away on my own before, and I hated being separated from my parents. I missed them very much and when I was alone, I often cried. Half-way through the month my mother came to visit me. When I confessed I was homesick, she hugged me, but said firmly, 'You can't hang on to my apron strings for ever. You must try and manage without me.'

And I did. Even when, a few days later, my big toe turned septic and swelled up like a ping-pong ball. Even when, bandaged up, I was forced to spend my days sitting in a wheelchair, watching everyone else enjoying themselves. I was determined not to write to mother, begging her to take me home, so I suffered in silence, waiting for my 'holiday' to come to an end.

One day a camp leader found me with tears rolling down my cheeks. She tried in vain to comfort me, then said, 'Your name is Vera Diamant, isn't it? As you are a diamond, those tears of yours must be real pearls.'

Her words made me smile through my tears then, and have done many times since, for they are part of all the bitter-sweet memories of those bygone days. They are indeed the pearls of my childhood.

When at last mother came to fetch me and exclaimed in horror at the sorry sight of me, I said proudly, 'I didn't want to worry you and anyway, I didn't cry. I only shed pearls.' Then I explained.

'You should have sent for me, but I am impressed that you did not,' mother said. 'I never realised you could be so independent. My little girl is growing up fast.'

It was this realisation which later gave mother the courage to send me away to an unknown country, and in so doing she saved my life.

Until that holiday in the summer of 1937 I cannot recall a single insecure moment in my life. I had sailed through those first nine years on the crest of a wave, being loved, being spoiled and, like any normal nine-year-old, taking it all for granted.

Even then angry threatening clouds were gathering on my life's horizon, but as the car sped away from the camp towards my home I was not aware of them, nor that my childhood was almost over.

In those days my home town, really no more than a glorified village where everyone knew everyone else, was a happy place with friendly, cheerful people. On either side of the wide cobbled street that formed the town centre, houses and cottages lined shady avenues and spilled into the countryside. There were two old but excellent schools for us children, and our pride and joy – a modern, well-equipped gym – was used by almost every able-bodied person in the town. Twice a week the gym equipment gave way to benches and the hall was transformed into a cinema; every other Saturday night both benches and equipment disappeared and the floor was filled with couples dancing to the music of the local brass band.

The town square was equally adaptable. Brightened by well-kept, colourful flower beds and shaded by majestic chestnut trees, it offered a peaceful refuge to the old folk on warm sunny days. But on Saturdays, with much hustle and bustle, the country market took possession. Stall-holders commandeered every available spot and housewives darted from stall to stall buying poultry, fruit and vegetables, while their menfolk conveniently disappeared into the two nearby inns for a tankard of beer, a smoke and a game of cards. Whenever the travelling fair came into town, it also set up on the square, as did the brass band on fine Sunday afternoons; and when not otherwise in use, the square's gritty, even surface made a perfect cycle track.

The surrounding countryside was a wonderful playground. As far as the eye could see there were woods, fields and meadows, and two rivers: the Jizera was ice cold, crystal clear and narrow, between steeply-shelving banks, shaded by graceful birch trees, and full of trout. We youngsters preferred the Elbe, which, though never the cleanest of rivers, was wide and warm. Its greatest attraction was that outside the town it branched off and spilled into a large natural basin with gently sloping sandy beaches. We proudly called it "The Lido", for it was ideal for swimming and bathers flocked to its banks on Sundays from miles around.

In late summer and autumn the woods were my favourite place. I loved their uncanny stillness, the feel of the velvety moss under my feet, the tiny, sunlit clearings strewn with woodland flowers, which made me feel as if I had entered some enchanted wonderland. To find a crop of woodland mushrooms hidden behind a tree always made my day. They were my father's favourite, so I happily rushed home with my find and proudly presented it to him. He used to say that no one cooked mushrooms like mother did, and when freshly picked by me they tasted like a dream.

My father had always wanted a son and when he was presented with me, his second daughter, he was more than a little disappointed. However, he became reconciled to my sex long before I did, for I was as much of a boy as any girl could be, more by nature than by any desire to please him. Cleanliness, as far as I was concerned, if it was a virtue at all, was an unnecessary and most boring one; I was a magnet to dirt. I was happiest in the company of boys. At first they barely tolerated me, but they gradually, though grudgingly, accepted me and even showed me some respect when I was the one who tumbled out of trees, was caught stealing fruit from orchards, fell into muddy brooks trying to leap to the opposite bank. I sought their company with dogged determination and was never discouraged.

Next to boys the passion of my life was cats. Wherever and whenever a furry creature gave me a hungry, forlorn look, I decided it must be lost or unwanted, and I smuggled it home. The warm loft above the storerooms of our wine factory was filled with soft hay for Vana, our horse, and provided an ideal shelter for my little strays. Some stayed, other made their way discreetly back to their own homes. This habit of mine was well known to the townsfolk and anyone in the neighbourhood who had lost a cat called on me before looking any further. Every now and then father raided the loft and left behind only the one which was my legitimate property; then there were tears and sulks and stony silences, but I soon 'forgave' him and started collecting anew.

I also loved horses. Nothing gave me more pleasure than to ride Vana bareback to the river, soap and a brush in my hand, to give him a really good scrub and then ride him back with his steaming prickly wet coat tickling my legs. My pockets were always bulging with sugar lumps for my four-legged friends – but I did not collect stray horses the way I collected homeless cats!

Vana's wet coat always reminded me of grandfather's beard, which was immaculately kept but very, very prickly.

Whenever I kissed him I had to stifle my giggles because it tickled unbearably. Grandfather was an imposing-looking man, stern and dignified with piercing eyes, but he had a heart of gold. He made his living as a businessman, but he was also a fine pianist and a politician – quite an awesome combination! Above all he was a family man and the highlight of his week was to see his son, daughters and grandchildren gathered around him on Sunday. The dining table in his large airy Prague flat seemed to extend to almost any length to accommodate the whole family.

Our cousins Honza and Tommy were nearly always there. The sons of mother's brother Gustav, they were roughly the same age as Eva and me, and lived near our grandparents' flat. Uncle Gustav was a lawyer, and a very clever man; I remember Aunt Marti as a woman of exceptional soft dark beauty. Both boys had been lucky enough to inherit their mother's looks as well as their father's brains. Though they were serious and well-behaved, they were great fun to be with, at times.

I envied my town cousins their composure, their good manners and the ease with which they wore their expensive clothes. I was always extremely uncomfortable in my Sunday best and it took all my will-power not to fidget or interrupt and to keep my food on the plate and off my lap.

Grandmother always sat at the far end of the table: a tall, erect figure with a beautiful face gazing at us with unseeing eyes. A tragic accident when she was in her twenties had robbed her of her vision. She carried her burden uncomplainingly and without bitterness; she was never clumsy and was so independent that it was hard to remember that she was so severely handicapped. Whenever I was alone with grandmother I had the uncanny feeling that she could see into my very soul.

My sister Eva coped easily with the family Sundays. Four and a half years my senior, she was a serious, studious girl, old and wise for her years. My tomboy childishness was a source of great irritation to her and she did her best to change and 'improve' me, bossing me about whenever she had the chance. But I was every bit as obstinate as she was and all her efforts met with dismal failure. Although we did not get on too well when I was very young and although I envied Eva her dark, classical good looks, her seniority and the privileges that went with it, she proved to be the best sister in the world when I really needed her.

There was a special closeness between Eva and father, and they would often go for long walks together, deep in some intimate discussion. Father loved us both, of course, but I was still a child to him – a rather naughty one at that – whereas Eva was old enough to be his friend as well. Father oozed good humour and had a strong sense of fun, but he had a quick temper which I all too often roused. He hated formality and relatives 'en masse' and I suspect that he disliked the Sunday gatherings as much as I did. His frequent absences from the long family table made that quite obvious even to a child as young as I was. But father was very fond of my grandparents and they in turn adored him: his natural charm and warmth, coupled with his rather roguish good looks, opened most doors and broke many a heart. He was equally popular with his professional and business friends and with the local country folk. He was always 'at home' on Saturday mornings to anyone who needed advice or just a sympathetic ear, and always ready for a round of cards or a game of chess with the locals at the pub.

I didn't envy Eva her special understanding with father because mother and I were so very close. *Maminka* . . . just the sound of the word brings back the feeling of being locked safely in her arms, memories of her gentleness, her inexhaustible patience and understanding. She was beautiful in everyone's eyes, but never more so than she was in mine. I cherished her with a fierce possessive love.

Mother had many admirers, but she had eyes for no one but father. In many ways they were complete opposites. She was as serene as he was temperamental, as reserved as he was outspoken, as elegant as he was casual. In spite of these differences, or perhaps because of them, theirs was a sound, happy marriage and Eva and I basked and thrived in its security and warmth.

Auntie Berta often came to stay with us. She was mother's unmarried sister who for years had been grandfather's right hand and grandmother's eyes. Mother and Auntie Berta were as thick as thieves and when they were together, father must have felt rather neglected. At any rate, I noticed that, as fond as he was of his sister-in-law, he usually had a pressing business trip to make when she came to stay.

I didn't like Auntie Berta very much then. She was so well groomed, so elegant, so clever . . . so baffled by my slovenly ways and manners. She often maintained that she simply could not understand how her sister could have produced a daughter like me. Needless to say, whenever Auntie Berta came to stay I did my best to keep out of the way. I was so fed up with being criticised, I wished with all my heart that I were bigger and older so that I could answer back! Come to think of it, the only thing I wished for in those days was to be more grown up. I longed to be shown the respect that my sister's years seemed to command, to be listened to occasionally, to be curvaceous and pretty instead of skinny and flat. I pictured myself with mother's beautiful hair which made a soft, glowing frame to her lovely face and fell in graceful waves over her shoulders when she brushed it at night. Why was my hair blonde and straight? Why hadn't I inherited her long legs and perfect figure? Why was I born with father's Jewish nose instead of mother's Grecian one? Why did I have his big ears? If I looked more like mother, I thought, then, perhaps, on our Saturday outings to the smart new restaurant in the woods, young men would come up to me too and ask me to dance. I was so tired of watching them queue up to dance with my sister, while my parents circled the floor and I sat fidgeting on my chair. More often than not I would sneak away and go down to the bank of the Jizera river. When it was time to go home, father invariably found me up a tree or wading in the river, best skirt dripping wet, in a vain attempt to catch a trout. That, anyway, was far more in character.

I was happiest when Marta was allowed to join our family outings. Marta was my classmate, my best friend, 'my shadow' as mother used to call her, and a constant visitor to my home. Her father was the local cobbler and the whole family lived in one large room over his workshop. Whenever I visited them I marvelled at the enormous bed where the three of them slept, which almost filled the room. Marta's mother was a large woman with a smile to match, and could conjure up dishes fit for a king. The taste of her feather-light apricot or plum dumplings is one of the most delectable memories of my childhood years. My mother too was a fantastic cook, and I still dream of some of her mouthwatering concoctions, but those fruit dumplings were in a class of their own.

When we were not playing outside, Marta and I had the run of our spacious flat. Mother worked several hours a day in the office, so we were often left to our own devices, with only our elderly maid to supervise us, but I could always twist her round my little finger. There was just one room which was out of bounds, so of course we sneaked in at every opportunity. The room had its own outside entrance and was large and impressive, with a wall of windows and a balcony overlooking the main street. The other walls were lined with beautiful hand-carved cabinets, which housed father's extensive library and mother's precious china and glass collection. The oval table seated twelve and was used mainly for business entertaining and special events.

Father told us once that the dining-room suite had been hand-made for a French count as a wedding gift to his fiancée, but she died in an accident just before the marriage. I used to fantasise about the romantic figure of the French count and his tragic bride.

Marta and I loved to tiptoe in, to slide along the highly polished parquet floor, to stroke some of those 'untouchable' expensive ornaments, to tinkle on the grand piano which adorned the far corner of the room and which none of us knew how to play.

Marta was a Catholic and none of my other friends, except for Jirka, our neighbour's son, were Jewish. Come to think of it, there were not many Jews in our town – religious differences seemed so unimportant in those days. We were not an observant family and only went to the synagogue occasionally. I was quite happy to join the odd lesson at school on Christianity (there was no Jewish instruction, there were too few of us). As far as I was concerned there was only one God and it didn't matter whether you attended church, chapel or synagogue.

To me then, being Czech mattered far more than being Jewish, for I loved my country and I was fiercely proud of being born a Czech.

Right from the time I was old enough to understand, I was taught never to take freedom for granted. Freedom was, after all, a luxury my people had been forced to live without for three hundred years. The independent democratic republic of Czechoslovakia had only been founded in October 1918 – ten years before my birth – after the disintegration of the Austro-Hungarian empire.

I was a child of the first generation of the new republic, when my country was still pulsating with joy and excitement, when freedom was still a rare and precious gift. At home and at school we were taught to be proud of being Czech, to love our homeland and our language (which for so long had come second to German), to appreciate our authors, philosophers, artists and musicians whose works mirror their love for their homeland, the struggles of their people, the yearning for freedom and the joy of freedom won at last. One only has to listen to Smetana's 'Ma Vlast' ('My Country') – it is all there.

I was lucky enough to have a wonderful teacher who took our class right through junior school. She was a born teacher, with the patience of a saint, who managed to get the best out of us and to inject us with her patriotism and enthusiasm. A wonderful story-teller, she made our culture, heritage and history into one long, always fascinating fairy tale, and like all fairy tales, it had a happy ending. She also made us aware that it would be up to us to write further chapters of the story, for we had a vital role to play in the future of our new democratic nation.

Our exposed position in central Europe made us strategically important too; we were sometimes referrred to as 'an island of peace and order' in the heart of Europe. And peace and order was kept by the head of our nation, *taticek* (daddy) Masaryk, the founder and first president of the republic. The son of a simple coachman, he had risen to prominence as a renowned university professor and an important figure in political life. During the First World War, and even prior to it, he fought the policy of suppression, defending the cause of the Slavonic people, particularly in Great Britain, France and America. Masaryk was a dedicated and uncompromising fighter for truth and freedom and earned the respect and devotion of his people. His motto 'Truth will prevail' hung on our classroom wall next to his portrait. We loved *taticek* Masaryk more than anyone; we placed fresh flowers under his portrait each week and never forgot him in our prayers. He was an almost legendary figure, and sitting tall and erect astride his horse. he looked to me every bit the shining knight in a fairy tale. When he died in September 1937, the whole nation mourned.

By then political clouds were already gathering on our horizon. I was too young to be afraid of words like 'Nazism', 'invasion', 'antisemitism', 'Hitler' – but I was disturbed by the sight of my parents' now often anxious faces and by the shadows which were slowly descending upon our house.

By the beginning of 1938 the shadows deepened and the clouds thickened as Hitler's troops set off on their march across Europe. Yet, even after the occupation of Austria, father remained confident and optimistic. Britain, France and the Soviet Union were, after all, our sworn allies, and Czechoslovakia was the stronghold of western civilisation in central Europe. Surely they would not forsake us! As well as the support of our allies, we had our army which ranked with the best in the world. Besides, right was on our side, our cause was just and all we wanted was to live in peace. We had nothing to fear.

Father, however, decided to take certain precautions. He told mother to stock up with non-perishable food, and then arranged to have Eva and me baptised. Though he did not think that the Germans would invade, let alone conquer Czechoslovakia, he felt that it would be a wise precaution for us to enter the Christian faith. Though he was aware that Jews in Germany were being persecuted, he, like so many others, was unable to grasp the terrible implications for the whole of our race. And naturally, young as I was, I failed to understand how it was suddenly significant and even dangerous to be a Jew.

Despite assurances to the contrary, Hitler was not satisfied with Austria, and by September 1938 he was demanding Sudetenland, strategically the most vital region on the Czech-German border. Czechoslovakia's confidence that her allies would stand by their promises to help was sadly misplaced. They apparently chose to believe that the acquisition of Sudetenland would finally satisfy Hitler's greed. As the last hours of September ticked away, an agreement was reached in Munich: the Czechoslovak government was informed by the allies that it must hand over Sudetenland to Germany. This was to be our nation's gift, its contribution and sacrifice to world peace.

The surrender of the strongest belt of fortification in Europe did not buy world peace, only a little time. It also broke the will and the hope of the Czechoslovak people.

For me life went on as normal. True, our pantry and cellar were now crammed with extra supplies of food and warm clothing. 'Just in case . . .' mother used to say, 'so we won't go short.' As she always spoke with such a reassuring smile, it seemed as though we were all characters in an adventure story.

Then one day there was a new girl at school. She had no coat to keep out the October chill and no shoes on her feet. Anna was one of the thousands of refugees who, as the Germans marched into Sudetenland, had fled empty-handed into the comparative safety of the unoccupied Czech territory. She had been lifted from her bed by her father and carried away, wrapped in a blanket. 'We left in such a hurry there was no time to dress,' she explained.

This was my first real contact with a victim of aggression. I was suddenly shaken out of my smugness and belief that nothing could really touch or interfere with our secure family life. I felt ashamed. Ashamed of my nice clothes, my comfortable home, my security, when Anna had lost everything. Seeing that her feet and mine were more or less the same size, I impulsively took off my shoes and handed them to her. 'Please take them,' I said, 'I have others at home.'

During the break I ran across the square to our house to get another pair, expecting a scolding. But when mother heard my explanation, tears welled in her eyes; she hugged me tightly and told me to bring Anna home after school so she could give her some clothes.

The year of 1938 was drawing to a close. The uneasy lull gave a false feeling of safety. But to me and my friends there was the old excitement of seeing the first fall of snow and the knowledge that soon it would be Christmas. How I loved those winters at home! First there was the feast of Saint Nicholas, on 6 December. All the children crowded into the gym, where, to our delight, Saint Nicholas walked on to the stage, a large sack on his back, accompanied by an angel and a devil with a whip in his hand. The angel distributed little presents to the children who had been good, and the devil searched out the naughty ones, but somehow or other no one ever got a hiding.

My last winter at home is still a vivid and magical memory. The fairy tale look of the brilliantly white, thickly wooded countryside, the glitter of snow under the street lamps, the joy of skating on the frozen river and toboganning down the snowy slopes, with a steaming cup of cocoa welcoming us on our return home.

Even today I can almost smell the mouthwatering aroma of Christmas baking, the delicious cake, bursting with almonds and raisins, and the trays and trays of cookies mother always baked for Eva and me to give to those who were alone or sick on Christmas Eve. How we enjoyed doing this, and how they enjoyed being remembered!

What a business it was to select the carp for our festive dinner! Each year thousands were caught in lakes and rivers of Southern Bohemia and then transported to towns and villages throughout Czechoslovakia. Barrels filled with the live fish stood in front of every shop and store. What fun it was to poke my fingers into the icy water and, when mother's choice was finally made, to carry the victim home in a bucket, proudly placing it in a full bath tub, to keep it alive and fresh until the very last moment. They told me how delicious it tasted, wrapped in egg and breadcrumbs, served with a vegetable salad in thick mayonnaise sauce and a bottle of wine – a hot fish soup to start, and apple strudel to follow. Unfortunately I could never eat the carp, because by the time it was ready for the table, the fish had become a family pet and friend.

The Christmas tree fresh from the woods brought the heady scent of pine right into our lounge, and it was always exciting to open the presents under it, although by then I was too old and too Jewish to believe that it was baby Jesus himself who had left them there. Anna and her parents shared our meal, and there were gifts for them too. My parents' generosity and compassion made me appreciate even then the joys of giving and sharing.

I can still feel the touch of mother's hand as we walked through the silent streets under the starlit sky, hear the distant melody of Christmas carols, the sound of the sleigh bells ringing in concert with the bells of the little church. More than anything I still remember the warmth and security of her embrace and her soft voice as she tucked me up in bed at the end of a perfect day.

15 March 1939 announced itself with a snowstorm; it was an unusually bitter wintry morning, with heavy dark clouds. It seemed as if the heavens themselves were in sympathy with the Czech people, for on that fateful day Hitler broke his pledge to honour our new frontiers and invaded Czechoslovakia.

Waking from the fitful sleep of the young, I snuggled under my feather-bed for another nap and then suddenly became aware of strange noises floating up from the street. I turned my head towards the window and saw my parents and Eva standing there. Eva was clinging to them both; father's head was bowed into his hunched shoulders; mother's back was shaking with sobs. Sleepy and confused, I crawled out of bed and tiptoed to their side.

German armoured cars, motorcycles and tanks followed by line upon line of high-booted, marching soldiers were moving along the street, filling our square. And as the last remnants of hope and liberty were trampled into the slush, the stricken people of our town who lined the pavements bared their heads and with tears in their eyes sang the Czech national anthem 'Where Is My Home?'. And in my bedroom, our small family group held hands and sang with them; the whole nation cried and sang 'Where is my home? Where is my home?' because suddenly our home was no longer ours. The years of occupation had begun.

Father had a business appointment in Prague, but he did not go; mother did not go down to the office. We stayed in my room, the windows of which overlooked the square. The troops had thinned out, as detachments were sent to the surrounding villages. When we saw a soldier nailing a notice to the door of my school, our maid went over to investigate. She hurried back and told us, 'The troops are temporarily taking over the school, so there won't be any lessons for a few days.'

In spite of the gloom which had descended on our house, I was delighted at the prospect of an unexpected holiday, yet guilty and uncomfortable for feeling that way, particularly when I looked at mother's tear-stained face. But after all, I was only ten years old and I was still looking at the world with the innocence and optimism of the young; in a way, the day's events seemed more exciting than frightening.

Mother would not let me go outside, but to my delight Marta appeared. With pockets full of sugar lumps we went to talk to Vana in his stable and then we climbed the ladder into the hayloft to play with my cat and her kittens. Jirka, the neighbour's son, who was the only other Jew in our class, soon joined us. We tried to plan what we could do while the school was closed, how to make the most of our free time when we were not allowed outside the safety of our homes.

Towards evening, there was a knock on the door.

'Heil Hitler!' said an unknown voice, and a German officer walked in.

'I have been told that you have a large room with a separate entrance,' he said in German. 'I am here to inspect it. The Herr Kommandant needs it for his office.'

Mother, who had remained comparatively calm throughout the long, long day, now broke down. She swayed and backed away from the door.

'Why our house? Please, not our house!' she cried. 'There are bigger and better houses in this town.'

'Your house is central and very suitable. Now show me the room!'

'This will be ideal,' the officer said after inspecting our beautiful 'out of bounds' room – from now on, the room would be out of bounds to the whole family.

His business concluded, the officer became quite friendly. Taking the key, he said he would be back in the morning and, with a cordial goodbye and a smart 'Heil Hitler' salute, he turned on his heel and was gone.

My German was by no means perfect: in fact, German was the language my parents used when they did not want me to understand their conversation. But I had had a year or two of private lessons and, at one time, a German-speaking governess, so I was able to follow what was said.

Although I was baffled by what was going on and upset at my mother's distress, I could hardly wait to tell my friends that the commanding officer of all those troops was about to install himself in our house. The feeling of importance that this gave me conflicted strangely with my annoyance at the fact that a complete stranger – a foreigner, in fact an enemy – had the audacity to barge in and help himself to our best room.

The next morning the same officer reappeared.

'The Herr Kommandant wishes to see the whole family in his office at once,' he said, quite politely.

When we entered the room and I saw this Herr Kommandant sprawled in the seat father always took at the head of the table, his highly polished boots clashing with the colour of our highly polished floor, his heels digging into the lovely rug mother herself had made, his documents scattered all over our beautiful table, in short lording it over *our* property – I suddenly found the whole scene offensive.

'I hear that you and your family speak German,' the Kommandant said to my father.

'That is correct,' came the reply.

'Well, from now on I want only German spoken in this house.' There was a pause. Father looked the Kommandant straight in the eye.

'I am the head of this household,' he said, 'and as long as I am alive, my family and I will speak Czech, and German only when in your presence.'

The Kommandant stood up, walked up to my father and spat in his face. Father was six feet tall, erect, dignified and proud. Never will I forget his humiliation! I stared in horror, rooted to the spot, watching the saliva run down his handsome face.

'Never, never will I utter another word of German,' I vowed silently, and truly, from that day to this I have not been able to bring myself to speak that language again.

And that day I began to understand what the Nazi occupation was to mean.

The Kommandant did not bother us again; a few days later he moved right out of our town, and so did most of the troops. It seemed almost as if the events of that unforgettable day had been no more than a bad dream.

I bounced back with the natural resilience of childhood. I was back at school now, studying for the end-of-year exams. It was my last year at primary school. The following September I hoped to join my sister at her grammar school in the county town of Brandys. Quite a few of us were about to sit the entrance exam and I hoped I would pass. I was considered quite bright and my reports were consistently good. I was looking forward to this new phase in my life – the daily train journey with other students, new friends, a new school, being that much older and more respected . . . But I knew that I would hate to say goodbye to the little school where I had spent five happy years, and to the classmates who would be going on to attend the more practical, but less academic, local high school. Hardest of all would be the parting from the ever faithful Marta . . .

Looking back, it seems as though, after the invasion, life went on in a somewhat mechanical way, as if we were all just waiting, waiting for what would happen next, for the false calm to break and the storm to follow. Father was back at work, mother in her office; our Sunday visits to my grandparents resumed. I was allowed to play outside and to go about all my old pursuits. Only the ever-present anxiety on my mother's face was a constant reminder now that all was not as it should be.

The threat of war loomed over our heads, the whole of Europe was buzzing with rumours. But father was an optimist. He thought that there would probably be a war, that the Allies would win, and that it would all be over very quickly. Or maybe it could be averted altogether. As to the persecution of the Jews – the Nazis had so far left us alone.

'Why should they bother us anyway?' he said. 'We've been baptised! Let's hope that it's all a storm in a teacup.'

Mother suggested that perhaps we should all try to get away abroad to safety, but father did not want to leave his flourishing business and familiar way of life. He put the experience with the Kommandant to the back of his mind.

'We were just unlucky to have a German bastard like that in our house!' he said.

Mother did not make any further suggestions. She would have felt terrible leaving her blind mother and her father who was now very much an invalid.

'How would Berta cope without my help?' she said to me once, and then dismissed the whole idea.

But there were other ideas in her head.

Some weeks later the bombshell fell. The four of us were sitting round the table at dinner, but mother was not eating. Suddenly she pushed her plate aside, looked at father and said, 'I heard today that both Eva and Vera can go to England.'

There was a deathly silence. Father looked shocked and

terribly surprised. His eyes questioned mother, wordlessly urging her to continue.

'When I was in Prague a few weeks ago,' she said, 'I had a talk with my brother Gustav. Apparently there is an organisation in England which is helping Czech Jewish children to get away from here and into English families. He gave me the address of the Prague office. Gustav has registered both Tommy and Honza, so I went and put Eva's and Vera's names down too . . . and now they have been chosen. Their transport will leave before the end of July.'

Father still had not spoken, but all at once his dear face seemed haggard and old. He covered it with his hands, whilst we all waited in silence. Then he lifted his head, smiled at us with tears in his eyes, sighed and said, 'All right, let them go.'

This decision was to save our lives, but at that moment my overriding feeling was one of excitement at the impending journey mixed with not a little apprehension.

The date of our departure was put forward to the end of June, which sent the whole household into frenzied preparations. I gathered together my most precious possessions – my autograph book with its messages from family and friends, my favourite doll, my best books, my little Czech flag, the puppet my teacher had given me and my photograph album.

Mother, determined to send us away in style, took us on several shopping expeditions to Prague and kept the local dressmakers working overtime. We were allowed one trunk each, and they were filled with beautiful new clothes, most of which hardly allowed for growth. Father kept repeating, 'You'll be back within a year, you'll see!' Mother tried to believe this too. It was the one thought which gave them the strength to stand by their decision to send us away.

We all clung to that hope. If any of us had admitted to ourselves that our separation could be a lengthy one or that there was a possibility we would never see each other again, we could not have parted.

I plagued mother with questions: 'Who am I going to?' 'How did Eva and I come to be chosen?'

Mother could give only a vague answer. 'I took your photos to a tiny office in Prague, run by the British Refugee Committee. You should have seen the queues! I had to stand for hours. You'd be surprised how many parents want to send their children to England. They gave me forms to fill in, to give details of your background and hobbies, which were then sent to London. The people who have chosen you must have liked what they saw and read. I can't tell you anything about them, but they must be good caring people for wanting to help. All I know is that Eva will be living with a lady in Dorset and you, Vera, are going to a family in Liverpool. You'll find out the rest soon enough.'

There were some who thought mother heartless and cruel to send us to a strange country, to unknown people, when we could not speak a word of the language. Jirka's mother, oblivious to mother's inner torment, was particularly vehement in her criticism, and accused her of acting like a wicked stepmother. If that woman could only have seen into her own future, she would have fallen to her knees and begged mother's forgiveness for those harsh words, and blessed her for her compassionate, generous heart! In less than a year she was to die of a terminal illness, and later her husband was arrested and shot by the Gestapo. Mother then took Jirka and his little brother to live in her home, and she loved and cared for them as if they were her own.

I had said goodbye to my school, the headmaster, my teacher and most of my classmates. I felt terribly excited and very important. As far as I knew, no one from our town had ever been to England, which made me something of a celebrity. Anyway, I was sure I would be back home soon . . .

On the last afternoon a few of my special friends came to wish me a safe journey and a speedy return. Mother decided we should all drink to that and she brought out a bottle of Malaga wine.

Now, for as long as I can remember, there was always a

bottle of Malaga in mother's office. I was allowed a drop on
very special occasions, or when I was ill, for the wine was
supposed to have medicinal qualities. It was sweet, thick and
nutty and so delicious that I claimed to feel unwell as often
as I dared.

Marta stayed behind when the others left. 'You will come
and play with the cat,' I ordered, rather than asked, her.
'She's bound to miss me. And please don't let anyone drown
her kittens!' My cat was expecting another litter, and Marta
said that she would find homes for them all. 'Mummy will be
terribly lonely,' I added, and Marta promised to come and
see her every day. And she did, like the faithful friend she
was, even when it was forbidden for Christians to mix with
Jews. She came even when mother begged her not to,
fearing for her safety. She had given me her word, so
stubbornly and courageously she came every day.

We went into the stable. Vana was soon to leave the
household too, for the Germans had requisitioned him for
the army. I flung my arms around his neck and buried my
face in his mane; I kissed his nose and gave him a last
handful of sugar lumps. He too was embarking upon an
unknown future. And I knew I would never see him again.

That evening father gave me a beautiful leather-bound
book. To my surprise it was full of empty pages. 'What is it
for?' I asked. 'Use it as a diary,' he replied. 'I am sure you
will send us lots of letters, but it would be nice if you also
kept a record of your activities, thoughts and feelings. I
purposely chose a diary without dates, for there may be days
and weeks when you have nothing to write about, and other
times when you fill pages and pages. You yourself will know
when to write. Just think how lovely it will be when you are
back home and we can all sit together and relive your
experiences through your diary.'

When I was ready for bed mother came to tuck me in. The
excitement I had felt all day had now subsided. Looking
round my familiar room, seeing all the lovely things I was
leaving behind, realising that tomorrow I would be on my
way made me homesick before I had even left.

Mother, as if reading my thoughts, hugged me and said,

'There will be times when you feel lonely and homesick. That is only natural. But remember you are our precious brave little diamond and your tears are pearls.' She carried me in her arms to the window and together we looked out into the starlit night. Then she said, 'If the time ever comes when we can't write to each other, and even while we can, the sun and the stars which shine on you will be shining on us too, wherever we are. Let us make the sun and the stars the messengers of our love and thoughts. Through them we will always be close.'

The day of departure came, and the four of us, squeezed into the car with all the luggage, were on our way to Prague. The first stop was our grandparents' flat. How old and frail they seemed that day! Grandmother had dark circles round her eyes as if she had not slept for days. Her gentle hands lingered on our faces, as if she wanted to memorise each feature for ever; her blind eyes were filled with tears. Grandfather lifted me on to his knee and hugged me tightly. 'You are your parents' child,' he said, 'and I know we will always be proud of you.' He kissed me, and I didn't mind his prickly beard at all, and suddenly I wished our Sunday dinners, boring as they were, could go on for ever . . .

Outside the house we met Tommy and Honza. They were very excited as they had just heard that they would also be coming to England in a children's transport at the beginning of September. This happy news broke the gloom and strain of the day. 'See you in England!' we called to them as the car set off to the station.

Auntie Berta squeeezed in beside me. I felt her trembling, and sneaked a look at her face. It was pale and drawn, and lacked its usual cool composure. She seemed so . . . vulnerable. 'You will write often, won't you,' she said. 'Mummy will live for your letters, so shall we all . . .' And in that moment I realised how much she loved us and that her outward coldness belied her true feelings.

The station platform was filled with anxious parents, the train packed with excited children. There were tears, last words of advice, last words of encouragement, last words of love, the last embrace. 'See you again in a free Czechoslovakia!'

I cried impulsively as the whistle blew. My parents looked scared, and so did other people, as there were Gestapo men about. And as the train slowly pulled out of the station, in the sea of people I saw only the beloved figures of mother and father, their brave smiles vainly trying to hide their anguish.

There was a lump in my throat. I clenched my fists and screwed up my eyes to try and stop the tears. I felt a hand cover mine. I turned, and in Eva's distraught face I saw a reflection of all that I was feeling. We sat there in silence, united by our sadness, by our fears and our hopes. For the first time in my life I felt really close to my sister.

As if reading my thoughts, Eva said, 'You'll always have me. I'll be a poor substitute, I know, but you'll always have me. Promise you'll turn to me when you're sad, when you're homesick, when you need me. Never forget that I care.'

I knew then how lucky I was to have a sister like mine travelling with me to the Great Unknown . . .

2
'You Shall Be Loved'

THE FIRST TIME I opened the diary father gave me I wrote:

> ... I slept a little, then woke on the border near Terezin.
> We sat there for four whole hours, because the leader of
> the transport had forgotten some important documents in
> Prague, without which they would not let us cross the
> border. Then came Germany – a bit like Bohemia, but
> much uglier, though I must admit the mountains and the
> forests looked nice. Then came Holland – oh, it was so
> flat, and the houses all alike, the rivers wide, because they
> were soon to spill into the sea. And then, that same night,
> there was the sea. Even in the dark it was such a beautiful
> sight!
> We got on a big ship and went into our cabins to sleep. I
> wasn't at all seasick, but I woke up very early in the
> morning. Eva was already looking through the porthole at
> the first rays of the sun spilling over the sea. It was such a
> breathtaking picture. I crept to her side, she put her arm
> around me and together we watched the sunrise . . .

As I watched the first day of my new life begin, I
remembered mother's words and I sent my love and
thoughts to her through the sun – and I carried on doing so
right through the long years of the war.

So many details of that first day are imprinted in my
memory – our first English breakfast, which most of us fed to
the fishes; the journey on the early morning train through
the sleeping countryside, passing through towns and villages
which seemed no more than row upon row of identical red-
brick houses. Then at last we were in London, proudly
riding on a double-decker bus through the busy streets.

We stopped in front of a large gloomy hall, and were
ushered inside. There we sat in rows, with labels hanging
round our necks, waiting for our names to be called, all of us
suddenly subdued, apprehensive, wondering what was to
come.

As name after name was called, one by one the children left their places and went to a side door to meet their new guardian. When Eva disappeared through that side door I felt terribly alone. She sneaked back a few minutes later to press a piece of paper with her address into my hand, telling me to write as soon as I arrived at my destination. Then with a kiss and a hug she was gone. And I went on sitting there . . .

Child after child left the hall until there was no one but me. My turn never came, and there I sat in that huge empty hall, feeling utterly lost, utterly dejected, and very, very worried. 'Perhaps they don't want me, perhaps they've changed their minds,' I thought with rising panic. 'Whatever will become of me?'

Hours later, or so it seemed, the man in charge came over to me. 'It appears that your English family can't come for you until Monday,' he said, wisely ignoring the tears which I was struggling to hold back. 'I will take you to some nice people who help to bring children like you here. You can spend the weekend with them.'

The man led me to a chauffeur-driven limousine, and together we were taken to a beautiful house overlooking a park. I believe it was the home of a bishop, one of the sponsors of the children's transports. A butler opened the front door and handed me over to a poker-faced, starchy maid who ushered me into a lift and took me to an unwelcoming, formal bedroom on the third floor. The door closed behind her and I was alone. I examined the huge bed, the thick tapestries, and listened to the heavy silence. I was close to tears again. Then the door opened and a girl of about eighteen came in, smiling at me. 'Hullo, little girl. Is there anything you want?' she asked in *Czech*!

I was so happy to hear her that I wanted to throw my arms around her, but I resisted the impulse and bombarded her with questions instead. I learned that I was a guest of a very distinguished man who had twin daughters. Maria, as the Czech girl was called, was employed as their companion. She chatted to me while I washed and tidied myself before meeting the twins. I couldn't help noticing how badly Maria

spoke, and I asked with the directness of a child, 'Why is
your Czech so bad?'

'When you've been here a year like I have,' she replied,
'without ever having a chance to speak it, you'll probably
forget it altogether.'

I was horrified at the very thought. To return to my
parents able only to speak in broken Czech, or not to speak
Czech at all . . . that was unthinkable! I vowed never to let
that happen to me. I would not forget my language, not a
single word!

In fact, Maria was a refugee from Sudetenland, had had a
German education and had never learned the Czech
language properly. Nevertheless she did me a good turn, for
I took her warning to heart and became doubly determined
not to forget my mother tongue.

When I was ready, Maria took me to a drawing room to
have tea with the twins; she introduced us and then left. I
expected to meet other children, but to my astonishment I
was faced by a couple of tall, thin ladies who acknowledged
me with a warm smile, gestured me to be seated and then
proceeded to pour tea into my cup. I had never drunk tea
'the English way', and remembering the horrid taste of the
dishwatery liquid I was given on the boat, I pointed quickly
to the milk jug on the table. 'Oh, you would prefer milk,'
said one of the young ladies, beaming at me, pleased with
herself for understanding, and poured me a lovely glass of
cool fresh milk.

By then I was absolutely ravenous, for I had not touched
my breakfast and had eaten nothing since the previous day. I
helped myself to the wafer-thin brown bread and butter,
spreading the slices liberally with lemon curd which I
assumed to be a kind of honey. What a shock that first
mouthful was! I had always been a fussy eater with a very
sweet tooth and in spite of my hunger I found the
combination of the strange spongy bread, salty butter and
sharp lemon curd foreign and almost inedible. Whenever my
hostesses' eyes were turned, I slipped the bread slice by slice
into my handkerchief to be flushed down the toilet. When
they were looking at me I smiled, pretending to munch

away, so they would not think me ungrateful. My stomach rumbling, I longed for the rucksack mother had packed with food for the journey. Above all I longed for a slice of Czech bread. There was half a loaf in the rucksack, and I could hardly wait to get my teeth into it. 'I'll have a really thick slice, with lots of mummy's jam', I promised myself, and as soon as Maria reappeared, I asked her for my rucksack.

'It's in the kitchen,' she said. 'Come on, I'll take you there.'

In the basement kitchen the cook in his tall white hat gave me a big smile and a hearty handshake. But, horror of horrors, my rucksack was empty! Apparently the leader of the transport had said on arrival, 'Now we're in England, we'll eat English food. Throw all the Czech food away!' And the maids had obligingly emptied not only his bag but mine too.

I was so upset that I hardly heard Maria's explanation. My bitter disappointment was matched only by my indignation. I had always been taught that Czech bread was sacred; it was not to be wasted, and never to be thrown away. 'How could he do such a thing?' I sobbed, quite forgetting what I had done with my English bread.

That first night, alone in my austere bedroom, I sat by the window gazing into the sky. I ached with homesickness, homesickness for the familiar things, for my bright cosy room, the smell of father's spiced tobacco, the sound of his teasing voice, homesickness for everything that meant mother. '*Maminko,* are you sitting by the window too, thinking of me?' I whispered to the stars, and taking out a pad and a pen, I wrote my first letter home.

The following Monday I was driven to an office and led into an empty room to await the arrival of my English foster parent. Before very long the door opened and there stood a little lady, barely taller than I was. Her hat sat askew on her head and her mackintosh was buttoned up all wrong. A pair of bright eyes peered at me rather anxiously from behind glasses before her rosy-cheeked kind-looking face broke into a wide warm smile. She ran towards me then, laughing and crying at the same time, and hugged me tightly, talking to me with words I could not understand. I was slightly baffled, not a little embarrassed and somewhat over-whelmed, but greatly relieved to be met by such a warm and jolly person.

Now, as I write these words, this same lady is ninety-two years old; she is smaller than ever, only four foot something tall, but her heart is still as big as a house. I asked her only the other day what she remembered of our first meeting.

'I was taken to a house in Bloomsbury,' she said, 'and shown into a big bare room. It was quite empty, there wasn't a stick of furniture in it, not even a chair. In the middle of the room was a little rucksack and a little jacket, and next to them a forlorn little girl. It was such a pitiful sight! I flung my arms around the little girl and said, "You shall be loved".'

And loved I was. I was very lucky with my English family . . .

Soon we were boarding a train bound for Liverpool. By then I knew that the little lady's name was Mrs Rainford, that she hoped I would call her 'Mummy Rainford' and also that she had a daughter called Dorothy. And she had learned from me that I had a sister, Eva, here in England. Eager to show off my knowledge of English, I proudly came out with the only other phrase I had learned and announced, 'I have hunger'.

At that, Mrs Rainford shot out of her seat and out of the carriage, shouting and gesturing for me to stay where I was and totally ignoring the guard who was poised to blow his whistle for the train's departure.

'I've been abandoned!' I gasped with rising panic. 'What if the train leaves without her? I don't even know the address I am going to.'

The train was already moving when she almost literally fell into the compartment, a dripping vanilla cornet held triumphantly aloft. I took it, thankful that she had re-appeared and thankful for the lovely creamy ice. It was the first food to pass my lips that I had really enjoyed since my arrival on British soil. What is more, I had to admit that it was every bit as good as Czech ice-cream, and maybe even better.

As we walked from the bus stop towards the neat little red

brick semi in a quiet cul-de-sac in Bootle, I ventured a shy glance at my English sister walking beside me. She had waited for us patiently at the bus stop for hours and had greeted me with the same spontaneous warmth and friendliness that her mother had shown me. Three years older than I was, Dorothy was also exceptionally pretty and had a pair of long thick pigtails that I particularly envied.

Soon we were in the drawing room and I was being introduced to the head of the family – a tall, slim man with a nice open face. Cheerful and pleasant, he seemed genuinely happy to welcome me, and so did the grandparents who had come up from the country for the occasion.

It had been a long, eventful day and now it was drawing to a close. My tenth year was drawing to a close too, for the next day was my eleventh birthday.

That night, in the privacy of my very own little bedroom, surrounded by my own familiar things from home, I wrote again to my parents. My excitement at the events of the day merged with the ever-present need to share my thoughts with my loved ones. Little did I know that mother had already received my letter and was about to answer it on my birthday:

>   Celakovice
>   4 July 1939
>
> My dearest, sweet *Veruska,*
>
> . . . Reading your letter, I rejoiced and I was filled with tremendous contentment, for I could see that my little *Veruska,* in whom I always had great faith, has not disappointed me even now and that I can be and that I am proud of my brave little girl.
>
> I wish you today, on your eleventh birthday, that happiness will always accompany your sweet self, that laughter and joy will be faithful companions of your youth, that steadfast faith in a brighter future will give you strength and that the thought of your parents, who love you so very dearly, will keep you as good and as sweet and as pure as you are now . . .
>
> Just remain good and grateful, my darling, to those who are looking after you so well.
>
> . . . The sun which is shining on you shines on us too, and through

that sun I am sending and shall *always* send you my love, my thoughts and an endless amount of kisses. When *tatinek* gets home this evening, he will write to you too.

Your happy

maminka

Father's letter came a day or two later.

Celakovice
5 July 1939

My little love,

You can't imagine how happy your beautifully written letter made me and I enjoyed every word. Your concern for our happiness is so touching. You have made today a very happy day and when we know where and with whom your permanent home will be, then we shall jump for joy! But the knowledge that both you and Eva are in the care of good kind people confirms my faith that you both were born under a lucky star and that you will always land on you feet.

You'd be surprised how many people in Celakovice have enjoyed reading your letter and how they praised you for writing so well and for being such a brave girl. Why shouldn't you be! After all, you *are* my daughter! By the way, your teacher read your letter and was as proud as a peacock! Let's hope you will even find the English food more to your liking in a little while . . .

Auntie Berta is coming to see us today, mainly to read your and Eva's letters, to copy them for the grandparents, so they too have something to be happy about.

I wish you lots of good luck and good health, my little love, and that you will find yourself with a truly kind family, and I look forward so very, very much to more news from you.

Your *tata*

The day after my birthday, which I celebrated in style with fresh strawberries and lashings of ice-cream, I went to school. That was an experience I shall never forget! Unlike the schools in Czechoslovakia, the English state schools had not yet broken up for the holidays.

Dorothy, bursting with the excitement of having a Czech refugee as a new sister, had spread the news of my arrival far and wide. In those days, little was known about Czechoslovakia and I think the children expected me to look like some creature from another planet. I am sure they were quite disappointed to find that I didn't.

As Mrs Rainford walked the half-mile to school with me, holding my hand reassuringly, the streets were lined with curious children who stared at me in utter silence. Perhaps I should have been flattered, but I felt terribly self-conscious and uncomfortable with the only sound that of our footsteps and so many eyes boring into my back. Once we arrived at the school, however, the children soon dropped their reserve and crowded round me. Since I had never been shy by nature, by the end of the day I had made many new friends.

To my indignation, I was put into a class with six-year-olds, though only to begin with, I was assured. It was felt that it would be easier for me to learn the rudiments of the language in that class, particularly as the teacher spoke German. Now, as I said earlier, I had vowed never to speak German again. I didn't have to: the teacher did all the talking and explaining and I just listened, but it did make my introduction to English that much easier.

Dorothy was my best teacher. Determined that I would achieve miracles, she spent hours and hours demonstrating the meanings of different words, phrases and tenses. I was equally determined to teach her Czech. I soon gave that up, although to this day she remembers a few short poems and little songs we used to play together on her piano. Dorothy and all her family did everything possible to make me feel at home and loved and wanted. When, years later, I asked Daddy Rainford what had decided him to take me in, he replied: 'I knew I could not save the world, I knew I could not stop the war starting, but I knew I could save one human being. Great Britain broke the agreement with Czechoslovakia, and the Jews were most at risk, so I decided on a Czech Jewish child.'

Čelákovice, July 9th 1939.

Dear Mrs. Rainford !

We feel gratly indebted to you for
your unexpected favour from the 5th inst., the re-
ceipt of which we acknowledge to-day with all our
heart. You can believe us, the first days, when we
did not know the destiny of our children, we lived
in a terrible anxiety and trouble. But as soon as we
opened your dear letter, all our sorrow and uneasiness
has been driven away directly. These last few days
we feel happier again knowing that our little girl
has come to your hands, into such an esteemed family
with a loving heart and kindly feelings. This is indeed a great relief for a mother who had to do a sacri:
fice and send her darling daughter far away. Our
good Lord in heaven may repay to you, dear Mrs. Rainford, and to your lovely Dorothy, all your Kindness
you bestow upon our child.

We live here in straitened circum-
stances, both our children have been educated modest-
ly, and we shall be much obliged to you when you will
continue educating Vera in the same measure.

We feel very sorry for that we are
not able to contribute in no way to the educational
acquirements of the little one, as we are not allowed
to send to England whatever amount of money it might
be. In your letter you say also, the Comitee perhaps
will take care of Verá´ s school-education free of
charge, and herewith we beg to ask you whether you
will be so amiable to settle this affair yourselves,
or are we to send a letter to the Comitee about
this business ourselves ? Please to tell us what
we ought to undertake eventually. We do not know
well the English character as for this matter and
should be sorry to do a mistake somewhers.

Dearest Mrs. Rainford, your words our
little girl is enjoying love in your family circle, have given us once more the faith in God and
we trust that better times will come again over us.
We have been so happy at reading your affirmation,
you are our goos friends, and we can assure you,
that our gratitude towards you is really great and
sincere. Every day we shall pray to God to keep up
your love for our child and your friendship for us
here.

In the meantime we remain, Dear Mrs.
Rainford

yours most sincerely

Karl & Irma Diamant

And Dorothy had picked out my photograph from among several others because she liked my smile . . .

My new family was anxious to write to my parents, to reassure them how welcome I was in their home and in their hearts. My parents also sent their personal thanks. Eva and I corresponded avidly as well, and so did our guardians who were making arrangements for Eva to come and visit me before the start of the autumn term. Eva's guardian was the headmistress of a boarding school in Dorset which Eva was now attending.

As for writing to my parents, in those first months before the war, I bombarded them with letters, and they answered each and every one.

To begin with my letters home were just newsy and loving. My parents reacted accordingly. 'When I read your letter I was so happy, I jumped for joy so high that my head nearly went through the ceiling', father wrote. 'And those beautiful photos! What a lovely sweet girl Dorothy is, and the goodness fairly shines out of her mother's eyes. I am going to frame the pictures and hang them over my bed, so I shall see the three of you every day . . . '

Now and then father gently lectured me. 'I am pleased with how you are behaving and coping', he wrote, 'but may I remind you to be always spotlessly clean? Don't forget to wash your hands and face, and if you can, bathe every day and clean your teeth morning and night. Make sure that you always look neat and tidy so that everyone will say "Look at that smart little girl!" You can't stay our little ragamuffin for ever! You will write how you are doing in this respect so I needn't worry about it.'

Weeks passed and I settled in happily; I was enjoying life in England, and the constant stream of letters from home made me feel my parents were a part of it too. As my confidence grew, some of my bad habits returned, and I started making demands, for more books, clothes and shoes, not to mention a loaf of Czech bread! I was particularly put out that my doll's extensive wardrobe had been left behind and she didn't have a change of clothes. I pestered mother to send them in every letter even though I knew how difficult it was to send anything from German-occupied territories.

In the end father stepped in. 'Vera', he wrote sternly, 'we are trying to get a parcel off to you, but it is high time you realised that it is almost impossible. Don't you understand Czech? How many times do I have to tell you before you stop the constant refrain "I want, I want"! You'd drive the whole of Celakovice round the bend just because your poor dolly hasn't got another dress or her own pillow! But we are doing our best, and if we get permission we will send everything, even the bread, though by the time it gets to you it will be as hard as rock and you'll only break your teeth on it'.

Miraculously, the parcel did eventually arrive; it contained everything I asked for, and presents for Eva and Dorothy. Only the bread was missing. It had been sent, but confiscated by Customs. Once again I was robbed of the chance of eating my beloved Czech bread, but at least I kept my teeth.

It was mother, of course, who moved heaven and earth to get the parcel off to me. She was always the practical one who remembered to enclose stamp coupons for my reply (father invariably forgot), and who tried to fulfil my every whim. Mother kept me well supplied with news of my friends and of our town. She worried about little things – what was I eating and whether I was eating enough, how did I communicate, did I practise on the piano, how I filled my weekends, my daily timetable. As soon as I mentioned that I wanted a photograph of her and father, and of Marta and the kittens, she arranged for the session with the local photographer to coincide with a visit from my grandparents and Auntie Berta, so I would have a photo of the whole family. Her letters were always full of love and encouragement. 'I dream of you and Eva every night', she wrote, 'probably because like you, I fall asleep thinking of you both. I am so thankful that they love you too. Don't be too critical, always be good, happy and full of hope, and learn to love the Rainfords; this is the best way to repay them.' And there was not a letter which did not include the words, 'Is the sun kissing you on my behalf?' or 'Are the stars delivering my love?'

As the weeks passed I made friends and gradually became more familiar with the new surroundings and way of life. Daddy Rainford and Dorothy took me on many outings. I particularly remember the sandy beach where I had my first taste of salty sea water. I preferred the taste that Dorothy introduced me to – that of chips, smothered in salt and vinegar and served in newspaper. Once I had tasted this unknown delicacy, I almost swooned whenever the smell of a fish-and-chip shop wafted my way, and I would spend my last penny on a portion of chips.

In the middle of August the Rainfords took me on holiday to Penscot, a little village in Somerset. Oh, the joy of having rolling hills and open countryside around me again! The skies were mostly blue, the birds were singing, the air was fresh and I could run, walk and climb trees and swim in the river to my heart's content.

The Rainfords were keen walkers and we covered miles and miles of the beautiful terrain. I liked to spend the warm, light evenings outside, reading my Czech books and writing home. I was so determined never to forget a single word of Czech that during all the years I spent with my English family I read the few books I had over and over again. As I rarely had other Czechs to talk to, I often held long conversations with my doll.

While we were in Penscot I had a dream which recurred persistently right through the war: mother and I were standing in our kitchen; she had an apron round her waist, against which she was holding a freshly baked loaf of bread. I could smell that bread as, ever so slowly, she cut me a large thick slice. I took the slice from mother's hand, raised it reverently to my lips . . . and woke up. I always woke up at that precise moment.

We stayed in a small guest house belonging to 'The Adult School' run by the Quakers. Both Mummy and Daddy Rainford were local preachers, and sometimes preached in Methodist churches. Each night one of the guests took the evening service. I still could understand only a very little of

Irma and Karel Diamant. This photograph of my parents, taken at the end of July 1939, did not reach me until war had begun

How happy family life was for us all in Celakovice before Hitler marched in!

Eva and I and our cousins Honza and Tommy — these photographs, sent to England, found us all foster homes. Eva and I were the lucky ones . . .

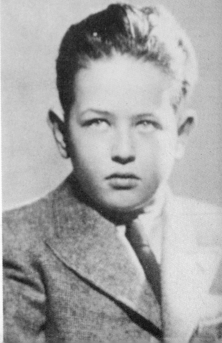

Eva came to stay at the Rainfords the week before war was declared. Dorothy is the one with the pigtails

what was said, but I joined in and said my own prayer. After all, there was only one God and I needed his help badly!

It was from Penscot that.I sent a very grown-up letter to my parents. By then the threat of war was greater than ever; I didn't really know what 'being at war' would mean in practical terms, and I hoped that if war did break out, it would be over quickly and would bring our return home that much nearer. But I did realise that while it lasted correspondence with home might be difficult.

I instinctively felt that a special letter was needed – a letter of love, as always, but one which would also show them that I was a big girl, and a sensible one at that, and *their* daughter, and that as such I would never let them down.

Mother's reply was waiting for me when I returned to Bootle:

. . . You can't imagine what joy your letter gave me. You are good and kind, you are my dearest little girl who has never let us down and never will. If only merciful God would grant us the chance to make up to you and Eva at least in part what we are unable to do for you now.

That your thoughts are with us, that your little heart flies to us, I feel this, my darling; why, there is not a moment when *tatinek* and I are not thinking of you. But we are glad you can see, experience and learn so many beautiful things.

We thank God that you are both with good people. Believe me, dear child, we now know that sending you away was the right thing to do. Promise me, that whatever happens, you will always be brave!

You have already learned, alas at such an early age, that life's path is not an easy one, that many wishes have to be set aside, unfulfilled. You must follow your life's path, my child, proudly and bravely, like your sister, your head held high, with determination and without fear. God will surely reward our patience one day with a joyful reunion.

Honza and Tommy have just visited us. They are to leave in about ten days. They can hardly wait, and are looking forward so much to joining you in England.

You are both my own, my very own sweet daughters and I am warmed by the knowledge that you are where you are . . .

Eva came to stay soon after my return to Liverpool. I don't think I have ever been as pleased to see anyone as I was to see her alight from the train. She was like a breath of home, a glimpse of mother and father. Her familiar face beamed at me, and I ran to her, shouting with happiness and excitement.

How the Rainfords liked her! For a fifteen-year-old she seemed so grown-up, so composed, and she spoke such good English! Eva told me how much she loved her school. It was rather grand, set in beautiful grounds, and everyone was kind to her. She had already made friends with some of the girls and their families, and had spent some of the holiday at the home of one of them, called Bunty. To my delight, Bunty's family had invited both of us to stay with them during the Christmas holiday. Eva told me their house overlooked Poole harbour, and that you could see the sea from the bedroom. Eva kept the best news till last: they not only had a cat, but a dog! I could hardly wait for December to meet them all, especially their pets!

Eva and I shared my bed; we talked half the night and all day. I stuck to her like a shadow, and even talked to her through the door when she was in the bath, or on the toilet! We wrote joint letters home and received joint replies. On 24 August father sent us a letter, part of which was in answer to my 'grown-up' one:

My loves,

I can't tell you what a pleasure it is to kill two birds with one stone and talk to both my daughters at the same time. I came home yesterday from my short vacation and, of course, the first thing I did was to read your last letters and admire the new photos. You seem to be putting on a little weight, Eva, you must be settling in well – you're becoming quite a young lady! But don't lose that twinkle in your eyes!

Thanks for the photos; I like the look of your friend and her house, I like everything, but most of all I like your letter which breathes of *joie de vivre* and enthusiasm.

From what you tell us and from what we read in the press I fear we have shod you inadequately. How could we have known that in England it rains for 185 days a year, is cloudy for 100 days and only fine for the remainder! And it is summer now; what will happen in the winter? Therefore we have decided to try and send you some strong, over the ankle lace-up shoes, which you will wear, like it or not. I have a feeling that when the real winter sets in you'll be glad of them! And, if you find you don't need them, you can always put them aside for a 'rainy' day!

Maminka sent you an address in her last letter. Memorise it, and also write it down somewhere safe. One day you may have to send your letters to that gentleman; he will forward them to us.

I can't tell you how your letter pleased me, *Veruska!* I am truly proud of you, my little love. *Maminka* has answered it so beautifully, and I too shall reply to it one day, but much, much later, when you are as old as Eva is now, for then you will be able to understand all I want to say – and I hope I will be able to do that face to face. For the moment all I need to tell you is that I cried with happiness, and swept *maminka* to her feet, and danced her round the kitchen. I can't tell you how necessary that letter was to me; it showed me what lies deep inside you, your fine character, sweet soul and your thoughtfulness. I waited and longed for such a letter, and I did not wait in vain. Perhaps all fathers are the same, they think their children are unique, and your letter proves to me you are. I still can hardly believe that my little *Veruska* was capable of writing such a letter, for it was written by a very sensible girl.

That you are enjoying yourself and having lots of fun is fine. I shan't even scold you for still climbing rocks and trees, but do be careful not to worry or annoy Mrs Rainford by being too wild or disobedient. Give your wildness and disobedience a rest till you come back home . . .

The photos I had asked mother to send me took a long time to arrive. Father enclosed a note with them. 'I want a smile on your face, and your head held high. That's my girl! Don't let the photos of Marta and the kittens, and of the rest of us make you homesick.'

I have these photos still. Marta, playing with the kittens; my parents with my grandparents and Auntie Berta; mother and father on their own. This last picture has the date 29.7.1939 stamped on the back, and I added underneath,

'This precious photograph from home came at the beginning of the war.'

In fact it arrived on 5 September, two days after the Second World War began. And their dear faces have smiled at me from that photo, which I still keep by my bedside, ever since that day.

Eva was still with me on 3 September when the news was announced that Great Britain was now at war. She looked grave and pale and she reached reassuringly for my hand. I could feel that all too familiar mixture of excitement and fear surging within me; I had no idea what effect the war would have on the world, but I knew that it would mean another drastic change in my life.

One of my first thoughts was not for myself, nor for my parents, but for my cousins, Honza and Tommy. They should have left Prague that very day, and I could hardly wait to see them. 'Will they make it now?' I worried.

Sadly, they never did. I learnt later that they actually boarded the train, but it was not allowed to leave the station. From that day on, all children's transports to England ceased.

3

Let This War Have
a Happy Ending . . .

LIVERPOOL'S INDUSTRY AND extensive docks made it a prime
target for German bombers. A mass evacuation of children
had already been planned, and was now put into immediate
effect. So, barely two months after my arrival in England, I
was on the move again.

Children from my area were evacuated to the outskirts of
Southport, a lovely seaside resort not far from Liverpool.

As it happened, Dorothy and I were very lucky, for
Mummy Rainford had a friend there who was willing to take
us both, so we did not have to go to complete strangers, or
be separated.

To begin with, I found the change confusing. After all, I
was just getting used to the Rainfords and their way of life,
and was now faced with another strange family with a very
different lifestyle. My new home was much larger than the
Rainford's, and more luxurious. It was exceptionally tidy
and clean, and it was made clear right from the start that it
was to remain that way.

I soon discovered that Auntie Margery, as the lady of the
house liked to be called, was a wonderful cook. Her crispy,
light Yorkshire pudding with lashings of syrup, and her
feathery, moist steamed treacle duff almost stopped my
yearning for mother's delicious meals; but it did not stop me
dreaming about Czech bread!

Life there was very different from life with the Rainfords.
Mummy Rainford had suffered from a weak heart all her life
and had to rest a great deal. She was never terribly
organised, and no one could have called her a fastidious
housekeeper; her house always had that untidy, lived-in,
comfy look. It didn't matter if I forgot to wipe my feet or
clear up after myself (the others didn't, anyway). Though
Mummy Rainford produced good wholesome food, she was

no great cook. Her biggest problem was that she had a slap-happy, undomesticated family, myself included, and that she was incapable of scolding, nagging, or organising us. She thought well of everyone and was exceptionally slow to anger. Her main aim in life was to spread love, and this she did, unobtrusively; her quiet gentleness brought happiness and comfort to all who knew her. She did not only teach religion, she lived it every hour of the day, and she still does.

Auntie Margery, by contrast, was a tall, plump woman with a smallish face framed by fine curly hair tied in a bun. She was extremely practical, highly organised, with a quick temper which I took care not to rouse. Her strong will and dominant personality made her the obvious ruler of the roost, but she too was kind, and active in the church and its good works.

At home I had always managed to twist mother round my little finger; Mummy Rainford's easy-going nature did nothing to introduce discipline into my life. But now I had to learn to live with it.

Actually, it did me good. I didn't mind too much, anyway, and conformed fairly quickly. Auntie Margery was proud of having a war refugee, and not just an ordinary evacuee, billeted with her, and she did her very best to make me feel at home. Her daughter Moyra, then in her early twenties, was a gentle girl with a keen sense of humour. Moyra's father was a shy man who, when not at work or at church, usually sat in an armchair behind a newspaper. He never had much to say, which was just as well, and probably why they were such a contented, close-knit family, for Auntie Margery was never at a loss for words and liked to be the spokesman for all three.

Here again they differed from the Rainfords, where it was Daddy Rainford who never stopped talking, there were always so many experiences and opinions he wanted to share with us. He was passionately interested in politics and world affairs and, like his wife, he did a lot of work for the church, particularly where children were concerned (I am the living proof of that). Worldly possessions meant nothing to him; I think he would have given his last penny to someone who needed it more.

Whenever I think of Daddy Rainford I see him standing in front of the fireplace, his fingers tucked under the lapels of his jacket, while talking into the night, putting the world to rights.

Dorothy invariably joined in. By no means a patient listener, she had very definite opinions of her own, and always had her say, usually at the same time.

Needless to say, Dorothy's strong will and forceful approach brought her into conflict with Auntie Margery almost from the start and I realised that it was only a matter of time before Dorothy either ran away or was thrown out.

There was another, very special member of my new family, Jill, a little mongrel bitch. I really cared for that little dog; I couldn't wait to get back from school each day so I could take her for long walks in the park, or across the marshes. I was determined to teach her Czech, and was thrilled when she learned to respond to a few basic commands. I liked to sneak her up to my room, which was strictly forbidden, and to cuddle her and tell her in Czech about my home, my horse and my cats. She was a more appreciative audience than my doll.

To my disappointment I had to attend the local council school, and not the grammar school as I had hoped. This upset me quite a bit since, after all, I had passed the entrance examination to a similar school in Czechoslovakia with flying colours. Unfortunately, the authorities would not take that, or my excellent reports, into consideration. They gave me a written test which I had no hope of passing after barely two months in England.

I was therefore very keen and very impatient to master the English language as quickly as possible. I pestered Auntie Margery and Dorothy with questions, my favourite phrase being 'Name please' which I kept repeating while I pointed to different objects.

Poor Auntie Margery even had to do her weekly bake with a Czech-English dictionary propped up in front of her, so that she could carry on a conversation with me. I used to get very irritated with her if she failed to understand what I was saying and I would tell her accusingly, 'My mummy would have understood!' In this respect Auntie Margery had endless patience with me.

That autumn I started to change shape. I arrived as a skinny eleven-year-old, rather tall for my age. Now I stopped growing upwards and started growing outwards. I was getting quite plump and developing hips and a bust! That was exciting in itself but most of my clothes were so tight on me that they began to split at the seams.

Auntie Margery saved the day. An expert seamstress, she let out what she could, and sold what she could not. As clothes and materials were on coupons by then, she could not buy me much, so she altered several of Moyra's dresses to fit me. I don't know if Moyra minded; I doubt that she was given the opportunity to say so if she did.

I hated Sundays. The Rainfords had never insisted upon my attending church. But Auntie Margery expected me to go to morning, afternoon and evening services every Sunday. And in between I was only allowed to play the piano, which I disliked, or to read, preferably the Bible, and certainly not comics, which were my newly acquired passion. I didn't know enough English to understand the Bible, and I never did learn to play the piano well. Auntie Margery's one concession was to let me take Jill out for a walk, which broke the monotony of the day.

During the morning and evening services I used to be terribly bored in church. I enjoyed singing the hymns, but I couldn't follow what was being said. So I daydreamed, fidgeted, and always played the same game with the numbers upon the hymn-board. 'This year, next year, sometime, never . . .' I counted, always hoping for the right answer to the same old question: when will I be back home?

On Wednesday afternoons I always took my time walking home from school because that was the day Auntie Margery had the ladies from her church to tea. She loved to bring me in to join them and to show me off. Her ruddy face beamed when the ladies complimented her on how well Moyra's old dresses fitted me and how they suited me, how healthy and plump I looked on her good cooking, how my English was improving with all her help . . . In short, how lucky this poor little refugee was to have found such a fine home!

I hated being on show. I know it was all well meant, but I was young and fiercely proud, and I wanted to shout at them, 'You should see my lovely home, you should have seen my lovely clothes! You should taste my mummy's cooking, you should see how she can sew! You should see my beautiful mummy . . .'

I had my own back though. The family said prayers before each meal and one day Auntie Margery asked me to say a prayer in Czech. With a straight face and without a moment's hesitation, I said, 'Dear God, stop this woman being so bossy and such a show-off! Amen.' It made me feel much better.

Contact with my parents was now difficult. Eva and I were able to write, but we had to send the letters to an elderly friend of Auntie Berta's who lived in London. He censored the contents, then sent them on to a business acquaintance of father's in Holland. We were given strict instructions about what and what not to write. We could not mention that we were in England and could not use English names. The letters had to be short, to the point and not too frequent. The replies which came were short and stilted too – with one or two exceptions. I felt cheated and I turned more and more to the sun and the stars and to God, as I could no longer write openly. And, of course, there was my diary:

2 October 1939

I have moved to a new family in another town so that I can live in safety. They have a car and we often drive out into the country to a farm which belongs to their friends, where we pick beans, apples and pears. I am well looked after, and I am enjoying myself. I go to school, I swim, I walk the dog, I keep happy and smiling. But at night, when I go to bed, my mood changes and I become serious.

First I kiss the Czech flag, hug my doll and the puppet my teacher gave me, then I make myself comfortable, look up at the sky and I pray:

'My guardian angel, please keep me safe. Bless *taticek* Masaryk, who surely is looking down on us from Heaven, bless president Benes, my daddy and mummy, grandpa and granny, my uncles and aunties, Eva, Honza and Tommy and all my dear lovely friends.. Grant them health and happiness. And please, let this war have a happy ending, let me return with Eva to my free country, to mummy and daddy, to all the good people I left behind, and let me find them safe and well. And please, make it soon.'

Maminko, tatinku, I send you my love and kisses through the moon and the stars. Just as a bright day follows a black night, freedom must follow oppression! Amen.

And with tears in my eyes I go to bed.

At about this time I received a letter from father which had been written before the war began; it took an awfully long time to arrive, but it is a letter which I shall always treasure.

My little love;

You, who are the younger, smaller one, I call my little love; *Evicka,* who is bigger and older, I call my love. Each of you has a small chamber in my heart which belongs only to you and into which no one else can enter. These two chambers are filled with love. Sometimes it is Eva's chamber which is the fullest, sometimes it is yours. Today it is definitely yours; I keep remembering and thinking of you constantly.

Maminka has gone to Prague for the day, and our new maid has gone for a walk, so I feel a little deserted. I had my usual nap on the sofa and I thought of you and what you were doing. One cheeky fly kept buzzing round my head, till in the end I jumped up and decided to get some exercise. I watered the flowers on the verandah, then I cut a chunk of bread and took it with a handful of sugar lumps to Vana. I made a fuss of him and told him

they were from you, and he neighed happily. I am sure he was
sending his love. Then I watched our three kittens playing on
the roof. They are big now, they drink milk from the saucer and
eat meat on their own, and next week they are leaving, all to
good homes.

I went out into the street, but instead of going for a walk I sat
down on the seat outside our house and watched the people
hurrying to the station. It has been a very hot week. The harvest
is in full swing and every farmer is rushing to have all his crops
under a roof before the weather breaks. And, as it is so lovely,
you can imagine the crowd that has come from Prague to swim
at our Lido. I am watching them now, as they pass on their way
home. Some look happy, others glum, depending on how they
enjoyed their Sunday. And I am enjoying myself just sitting here.
Every now and then a friend or an acquaintance stops and asks
after you and Eva, and they are pleased when I tell them all is
well.

I hope, little love, that my letter has cheered you. By the
way, we have just decorated the kitchen. I had intended to
have the toilet painted too, but you had written on the wall in
your own dear hand, 'Goodbye, my lavatory' so it will stay as it
is until you return. What a celebration we'll have then, won't
we?

As I read the letter, I did not know that I would take it out
and read it over and over again, until I knew it by heart. I
look at it now: the writing has faded and it still bears the
traces of my childhood tears. It was the last letter I received
from my father.

Life soon took another unexpected turn, which I described
in my diary:

                                        10 November 1939
My illness
A month ago I felt unwell at school. My throat was sore
and I felt all shivery. Auntie Margery made me lie down
after lunch and then she took me to the doctor. I was sick
there. The doctor told me to stay in bed until the end of
the week. That day and during the night I was sick eight

times. In the morning I felt much worse. Another doctor came. The minute he saw me, he knew! And after lunch, an ambulance came to take me to the scarlet fever hospital.

Auntie Margery looked worried to death and I thought I must be dying. But as the men put me in the ambulance, Dorothy ran out of the house and she said 'You'll be all right' and she was smiling, so I thought that maybe I wasn't dying after all. She shouted *'Na shledanou'* as they drove me away.

As soon as I arrived at the hospital and looked round my ward, I liked it. A large whitewashed room with eleven beds, with a window, a chair and a small cabinet by each bed. Two large tables in the centre, with flowers in the middle. A tablecloth was spread on one of the tables and four girls were sitting down, eating. The rest were in bed. They were aged between four and twelve years.

The nurse came. She washed me and gave me an injection. I liked the night nurse much better. I felt pretty ill at first, especially during the night: she often sat by my bed, and made me a milky cup of cocoa (in the daytime we always had it made with water). She was very beautiful, like an angel.

By the end of the week I made a good friend. She was called Jane. We kept throwing toys from bed to bed and, when the nurse wasn't there, we climbed out of bed. We also ate the most. The second week passed like the first. The pretty night nurse still made me my nightly cup of cocoa. Nobody knew; it was our secret.

After three weeks I was allowed to get dressed and to help around the ward, and to play games. I didn't want to leave the hospital, but the end of the month came terribly fast.

The last day in my beloved hospital

All the toys and books had already disappeared from my cabinet. Only my clothes remained. I had a bath, and I went to the kitchen and said goodbye to everyone there. Before long Auntie Margery came. It was hard saying goodbye to my new friends and the nurses.

We did a bit of shopping on the way back. The first thing I did was to write home.

Eva, thoughtful as ever, had not told our parents of my illness, which in those days was considered a serious one, until I was coming out of hospital. But as the war was on, and they did not expect frequent letters from us, they were not unduly worried at not hearing from me. Now we were both able to tell the truth and put their minds at rest.

I was not surprised to learn that Dorothy had packed her case and moved back to Bootle the very day that the ambulance had taken me away. Having not only shared my room, but also my bed, and having held my head through the night while I was being sick, she was immediately placed in strict quarantine. The thought of being confined to the house for up to four weeks and of having to deal with Auntie Margery without me to distract her attention horrified Dorothy. Their relationship, one of uneasy truce at the best of times, was usually explosive, so she used my illness as an excuse to make her escape and she never returned, probably much to Auntie Margery's relief.

I learned later that Auntie Margery was truly distraught when she found out how ill I was, and so was Mummy Rainford who, on hearing the news, rushed to the station and caught the first train without even stopping to take off her apron. Mummy Rainford in particular felt that I was her responsibility, that I was in England 'on loan', so to speak, and she was most anxious to be able to deliver me back to my parents in one healthy piece at some future date.

Both ladies were still very worried when, a week later, they came to see me in the isolation hospital, to peep at me from outside through my little window. They soon relaxed when they found me turning somersaults on my bed . . .

Now I was out of hospital, but still in quarantine and confined to the house. I was bored to tears, missing the hustle and bustle of the ward and the other girls. So I was delighted when Desmond came to see me. Auntie Margery didn't want to let him in, but he ignored her dire warnings and ran up the stairs to my room. An easy-going, good-natured seventeen-year-old, Desmond was Moyra's cousin who always managed to brighten my day.

Desmond invariably breezed in like a breath of fresh air, and his charm usually worked like a dream, even on Auntie Margery. I often found myself in the back of his old banger driving to somewhere exciting like the local cinema, or the huge new swimming pool in Southport, and on very special days to the fantastic fairground in Blackpool.

It was kind of Desmond to take pity on a doting eleven-year-old, to give me so much of his time, to buy me my first shaped swimsuit because I was falling out of the one I brought from home. No wonder he was my knight in shining armour!

Unfortunately, I did not repay Desmond's kindness very well, as witness some short entries in my diary:

Friday 16 November 1939

I've been sewing and tidying my cupboard and playing with the dog. This evening Desmond came to see me again. We played lots of games and listened to CZECH MUSIC!

Saturday 17 November 1939

Auntie Margery went shopping and bought wool so I can knit Eva a jumper for Christmas.

Dear God, I know you are now giving us the chance to win back our freedom. And I believe that I shall return soon to my parents and friends. Couldn't you please make it this Christmas?

Sunday 18 November 1939

Daddy Rainford came to see me; he brought me stamps and fruit. Desmond came after tea; he didn't talk much because his throat hurt.

Monday 19 November 1939

I didn't want to wake up this morning. I had a dream that Eva and I were in the children's holiday camp by the river at home; father came to fetch us, his arms filled with presents. It was such a beautiful dream, I didn't want to wake and face reality.

When I did wake up, it was to the news that Desmond had caught my scarlet fever!

Tuesday 20 November 1939

The war in Poland is over; Germany is the victor. In France there is fierce fighting. In Britain the war is just beginning. British and German boats are being sunk. Thousands of Czechoslovak soldiers are fighting with foreign forces against Germany. German is taught in all Czech schools.

Wednesday 21 November 1939

I spent the morning knitting. This afternoon Auntie Margery took me to visit Desmond in the isolation hospital. I felt quite guilty to see him there, but he didn't blame me a bit. I was the only one allowed inside! I ran to my old ward, and all the girls and nurses were pleased to see me.

In Bohemia the Czechs are fighting the Germans. Dear God, please keep mummy and daddy safe!

Thursday 22 November 1939

I walked the dog again, and this afternoon I was allowed to go shopping. In the evening I listened to the radio, and I sewed. I heard that in Slovakia the Germans are taking away shops and businesses from the Jews, and that German soldiers are just everywhere.

Friday 23 November 1939

This morning I took Jill to the little park, this afternoon to the big park.

President Benes is now in France. I firmly believe he will lead us to victory, like Masaryk did in the past.

I keep thinking how wonderful it will be when I am back home, with mummy and daddy. Dear God, please grant our nation freedom. You would make us the happiest family in the happiest country.

Sunday 25 November 1939

From today I am out of quarantine, so it is back to church.
After lunch I sat down to write home. It is so difficult! I
want to say what I think and feel, but I can't, I have to be
so careful, so I prefer not to write at all.

I wrote lots of other letters, to Eva, to Desmond, to the
Rainfords.

I tried to copy Hitler's picture. I only got his moustache
right.

Christmas will soon be here. Every child has a special
wish, and I am no exception. If I was given thousands of
the most wonderful expensive presents, and among them
was just a simple note which said 'the war is over,
Czechoslovakia is free', that would be the only present I'd
look at, the only one I'd want – the best present I could
ever have.

Deep down I knew there was no chance of being back
home for Christmas – but what would life be without dreams
and without hope?

In mid-December I received a surprisingly long letter from
mother. Concerned as she was to learn of my illness she was
unable to keep the letter short and to the point:

21 November 1939

My little *Veruska,*

I hope that by the time this letter reaches you, you will be well
and happy again. But if you are not yet completely recovered,
do not be sad, my darling. Play with the toys you have there,
tell them what life is like here at home where you are loved so
much and are constantly thought of. And believe me, my child,
that the time will come when we are together again. So be
happy and be patient and don't let yourself be homesick.

You will be surprised to hear that we have let your school use
our large dining room as a classroom, for they are terribly short
of space. I can hardly wait for tomorrow when the lessons start; it
will be so nice to have children around again.

Today the frost is sharp, but the sun is shining and bringing your love. It seems as if the sun is particularly bright, as if it wanted to say 'today your Vera is sending you her love and happy thoughts – be happy with her'! Each night I look at the stars and they seem to be whispering 'Have faith'. Yes, we have faith. So, my darling children, be healthy, be happy! Believe me, we know now that sending you to those good people was the right thing to do. Remember us to all of them, tell them how much we love them and how we pray for their happiness. Kiss Dorothy from us and, if you are well enough, and if you are able to, please write. We shall just have to be patient for now, and content with our memories.

Much, much love and thousands of kisses,

Your *maminka*

This letter from mother had to last me a very long time . . .

4
One Must Never Give up Hope

THE AIR-RAIDS had not yet started, so I went to spend my first Christmas in England with the Rainfords in Liverpool. They did their best to make it a happy time, spending far more than they could afford on presents and outings. I tried not to miss home too much and cheered myself with the thought that early in the New Year I would be visiting Eva's new friends.

What a wonderful visit it was too! Bunty's gracious house, with sweeping lawns and fabulous views across the harbour more than lived up to Eva's description, and I felt at home with the family straight away. The two weeks there flew by – days filled with lovely walks, family games played round the big dining room table or by the fireside, visits to their many friends and relatives. Most of all I enjoyed the company of Watch their sheepdog and their fluffy cat Keiller, which I was even allowed to take to bed!

And, of course, I had Eva. Now that the contact with our parents was virtually non-existent, she was like a little mother who wanted to know everything I had been doing and feeling; she was gradually taking over mother's role.

Eva had grown more serious than ever. I often found her sitting on the floor by the open fire, staring silently into the flames. This prompted me to write in my diary:

Eva is always staring into the fire. When I asked her why, she said 'Just look at the fire: one moment the flame is shooting up high, the next it dies down, but a spark always remains. Hope is like that flame – one moment it is strong, the next it nearly dies. But there is always a spark left. One must never give up hope. Freedom will come in the end.'

I like that very much.

When Eva returned to her boarding-school, I went with her.
The two weeks I spent there had a very unsettling effect on me.
And no wonder; there was a vast difference between my council
school, now housed in a dismal church hall, and the grandeur of
Eva's school. Ours was a makeshift arrangement because of
wartime shortages of teachers, facilities and equipment.

Now I found myself in a boarding-school seemingly
untouched by war and restrictions. Everything about it was
in total contrast to what I had known: the gracious buildings,
the rolling grounds, the excellent staff, the expensive
uniforms . . . It was like another world.

I remarked upon this in my diary: 'It is so wonderful here!
I love the life in this school and wish I could stay here for as
long as I have to be in England.'

But I knew that at the end of January I would have to
leave. The parting was terribly hard. Back in Bootle, I wrote
in my diary:

The days with Eva flew by. Before I realised, it was
Wednesday. Oh, how I hated that particular Wednesday for
being so impatient to get here! I knew I didn't have a hope
of stopping it. Yet there was a pleasant surprise for me when
it did arrive. On Tuesday, as I was packing my case, I
glanced outside and saw that it was snowing. So instead of
packing, I looked up to the heavens and begged God to send
down lots and lots of snow so that no one could travel all the
way from Liverpool to fetch me.

A little later Eva came in. I was surprised to see her, for it
was an unusual time for her to be out of class. She beamed
at me and said, 'Vera! Mrs Rainford can't come for you, the
roads are too bad!'

No news could have pleased me more!

Unfortunately, my departure was not delayed for long;
she came on Friday, and on Saturday I had to leave. I
thought my heart would break . . .

After breakfast on Saturday I ran into the school
building to say goodbye to the girls. I was almost in tears.
A car came to take us to the station and on the way I

couldn't stop crying. Eva tried to console me though she too was near to tears.

Darling Eva! How she encourages me and guides me when often she herself is in need of encouragement and advice. There isn't a better dearer sister in the whole wide world!

The train was already in the station. I burst into a flood of tears the minute Eva disappeared from sight and I cried and cried. We travelled the whole day. The journey that had seemed so beautiful when I was on my way to Eva was so horrid now that I was going further and further away from her . . .

I wrote to her as soon as we reached Liverpool.

Back at Auntie Margery's for the new school term, I soon settled down to my routine. Now that my English was much improved, I scanned newspapers and magazines, and listened to the radio, in case there was some news of Czechoslovakia, or anything connected with it. Whenever any Czech music was played, I almost wept with joy. Whenever Czechoslovak forces were mentioned, my heart swelled with pride. These men were my personal heroes, for they were fighting for the freedom of our country and for my return home.

I was aware that as early as autumn 1939 the Czechoslovak exiles in France had begun to form military units. They were led by Dr Eduard Benes who in 1935 had succeeded Masaryk to become the second president of the Czechoslovak republic. Benes was a great scholar and politician who had fought at Masaryk's side during the First World War. Now in exile, Benes headed the fight for freedom yet again, and the hopes of thousands of refugees like me were pinned on him. I saw him as an almost godlike figure and I prayed for his safety nightly.

Fully aware of my longing for all that was Czech, and in particular for other Czechs, the Rainfords and Auntie Margery did some investigating. Daddy Rainford found out that a refugee meeting or a concert was occasionally held in a Liverpool hall. Once or twice I made the journey and no one turned up but me, which was bitterly disappointing, but other occasions more than made up for that. In March 1940 I described a meeting in my diary:

Dorothy and I went to a small get-together of refugees from Czechoslovakia, Austria, Poland and other countries. First they sang Austrian songs. Then they recited a CZECH POEM AND SANG CZECH SONGS! Oh, how wonderful it was to hear the sound of a Czech song in a foreign land.

I haven't the words to describe how I felt as I listened . . .

During the interval I met a Czech gentleman who invited us to lunch the next day, which was Sunday. He ran away from Czechoslovakia to Poland where he was imprisoned, but he managed to escape a second time.

When I got to bed that night, and very late it was too, I was so excited I couldn't sleep.

Sunday – Feast day

We went into town and found the hostel where some Czechs were living. We had lunch: first came soup, then meat and fruit. There were about eleven Czechs present. Afterwards one of them showed me several manuscripts. I couldn't understand them really. Then came tea:

CZECH BREAD

and fish. I didn't have the fish. I only wanted the bread, and I wanted to eat it dry. That was more delicious than any feast!

Afterwards we went home and I did my homework and now I am ready for bed. Goodnight, little tummy, you've had a great day, haven't you!

Such occasions were a tonic to me, but they were very rare indeed.

Around that time I began to hear disturbing rumours that the Germans were ill-treating Jews in Czechoslovakia. As yet the horrors of concentration camps were still unknown and unimaginable. The persecution was of a milder form:

businesses, shops and properties were being confiscated; certain freedoms were withheld; Jewish children were not allowed to attend schools; Jews were being treated as inferior beings. That was all I knew.

It didn't make much sense to me. I could not imagine anyone wanting to persecute innocent people like mother and father. Surely they would be spared! But what if the Nazis took away our business and our home? Somewhat confused, I wrote in my diary:

> Dear God, there is something I am finding so hard to understand and I am looking to you for comfort and help. On Sunday I listened to the news and I heard how badly the Jews are being treated at home. I thought of mummy and daddy, and how they are coping. We haven't heard from them for such a long time. Yet even without the letters they are with us constantly. We feel their presence and I think that they feel our presence too.
>
> It occurred to me that when I return home I shall not be what I was before – that most probably I'll be poorer than Marta, poorer than all of my old friends. But I shall hurry back gladly, even to the poorest household. It will be cosier than the grandest mansion in England. And even if we don't have the money for coal, it will be filled with love and warmth because it will be our home in the most beautiful country in the world . . .

It was hard for me to cope with the fear that our parents might be suffering in any way, and it was only natural that I should turn to my sister for reassurance.

In my eyes Eva had changed from a bossy, rather irritating big sister to a person of almost saint-like qualities whose word was now gospel and who was the most important person in my world. I was missing the comfort our parents' letters gave me; I felt even more insecure now that I realised they might be in danger. I was bewildered, for try as I might, I could not understand. Why them? What is wrong with being a Jew? What has that got to do with the war?

The brief and infrequent notes received from home did nothing to restore my confidence.

Eva did her best, and she continued to do her best all through the war to protect me from pain, to soften the blows, to make sure I never lost faith in the future.

'Try not to worry', she used to write. 'Be happy, have fun, work hard at school and always believe that all will be well. That is what *they* would want you to do, and that is how you can please them most.'

I worshipped my sister and worried about her too – in case she was studying too hard, feeling homesick, or ill. One day that spring I wrote in my diary:

Dear God, I have so much to say to you tonight. I am so very worried. I haven't heard from *Evicka* for such a long time. It is, in fact, only five days, but it seems like years. If she hasn't written because she has to study hard, I wouldn't mind. But there's an epidemic of measles at her school. It isn't a particularly serious illness, but a very contagious one. And I am so afraid she may catch it. God, you hold the whole world in your hands; please, could you make sure she doesn't get the measles? After all, she is such a special splendid person – no one else has such a sister like mine and no one could wish for a better one.

I needed cheering up. Then one day something wonderful happened. When I came home from school, Auntie Margery greeted me with a big smile. 'I have a lovely surprise for you,' she said, unable to hide her excitement and pleasure at being the bearer of good news. 'I found a little Czech girl, the same age as you, living in Lancashire. Her name is Olga.'

I couldn't believe my ears. In all those long months I had been in England, the only compatriots I had met – apart from Eva – were grown-ups, and mostly old. Except for a pair of twins, but they were mere toddlers and couldn't even talk. But now – a girl of my own age! It was almost too good to be true.

Auntie Margery took immediate action and invited Olga for the weekend.

A shy, dark-haired girl with a freckled face, a year older than me, she was as excited to meet me as I was to meet her. Her shyness soon disappeared as we talked – and how we talked! We slept in the same bed and chattered into the night, doing our best to keep each other awake.

I learned that Olga was Jewish too, and had left her parents behind. She was living with a very religious Methodist couple, and had to attend all the Sunday services and play the piano! Olga came from Prague on the same children's transport as I had, and now lived in a small village where her 'adopted' father was the headmaster. She had made friends, but she longed for one that was Czech. We were so happy that weekend to have found one another! Our friendship seemed so very special – and it has remained so to this very day.

News of the war was now very grave. It seemed as if no one could stop Hitler marching across Europe, conquering country after country, forcing the Allied forces to retreat. With the fall of Holland on 15 May 1940 the vital link with our parents was severed. From then on we did not receive even the briefest of notes from home.

The last one had arrived a few days earlier. I wrote about it in my diary:

> At school I boasted to everyone that I had news from home. A letter from mummy and daddy! Yuppee! Hurrah! Nothing could have pleased me more. When I went to bed that night I said an extra prayer for them and I thanked God a thousand times.

In France, the British and Allied armies retreated to Dunkirk, bombed and machine-gunned by the Luftwaffe and pounded by artillery fire. Meanwhile, every available boat in the south of England – fishing boats, pleasure steamers, private yachts – put out to sea together with all available ships of the Royal Navy. Towards the end of May these boats rescued 338,000 troops from the beaches of Dunkirk.

The Czechoslovak troops fled to Britain too, and quite a few were wounded. Some were taken to hospitals in

Liverpool. This gave me the opportunity to contribute a little to the war effort. Obviously most of the Czech soldiers did not know anyone in England. And those in hospital were lonely and in need of a friend.

Glad to be doing something positive at last, with Dorothy's help I contacted the Liverpool hospitals and offered to visit any wounded Czechs who cared to see me. After all, to me they were heroes, and I felt honoured and proud to be needed.

Soon I was making regular visits to the hospital wards. The men were always pleased to see me, once they got over the surprise that their visitor was only a slip of a girl.

As shyness was never in my nature, and as by then I thought I knew everything there was to know about England, I chatted away as if I had lived here all my life. But I badgered them too, for details of their escape from Czechoslovakia, about the front, about everything. Sometimes I was asked to write a letter in Czech, or even to compose one in English. That made me feel very grown up and important. Some of the patients were anxious to get word to their families in Czechoslovakia through the Red Cross that they were alive and safe.

Some of the soldiers were too ill to talk. I remember one particular man – he didn't seem all that ill the first time that I saw him, in fact he joked with me, and called me his 'little imp'. But his condition worsened, and I realised that he was dying. In the end I was told not to go into his room, but I sneaked in and just sat there, holding his hand. I was very frightened, but I didn't want him to feel alone; how sad it seemed that there was no relative, no friend, just a small eleven-year-old sitting by his side.

France had such horrific memories for most of the soldiers that they did not want to talk about it. But there was one man, a jovial friendly young soldier, wounded in the leg, who was willing to describe some of his experiences. The men in his unit had been issued with only eight bullets each, he said, so all they could do was to use them up and run. Many of his comrades had been hit and killed or captured. 'I only made it because two of them dragged me to a boat,' he said, and added, 'I suppose while this was going on, you were busy playing and enjoying yourself, you lucky girl!'

I replied rather smugly that actually I had spent most of my free time knitting socks for soldiers. At school we were given a target and the girl who knitted the most pairs would be given a prize at the end of term. 'I'm sure to win it,' I said with confidence. 'I knit twice as fast as everyone else, but of course the Czech way is much better and faster than the English way.'

As it happens, this time I was right. The 'Czech' way, which in fact is the method used all over the continent, is much faster.

On impulse, I brought the soldier a pair of the hand-knitted socks the next time I visited. He thanked me, the smile never leaving his face. 'You won't mind if I wear them one at a time,' he said. 'You see, they had to amputate my left foot.'

I happened to meet this same soldier some time later when he was convalescing. He had been told, though he hoped it was only a rumour, that after his escape the Germans had selected twelve officers and ten men from the captured Czech units, transported them to Prague, and executed them in the Old Town Square. This incident prompted me to write in my diary:

> Even if it were true, even if the Germans had executed all these men as a warning to others, how glad they must have been to die in their own country rather than be shot in a foreign land!

The mood in Britain was sombre too. Chamberlain had resigned, and Winston Churchill was the new Prime Minister. I shall never forget his incredible voice on the radio when he made his famous speech after Dunkirk after he had refused to negotiate peace terms with Hitler: 'We shall fight on the beaches, we shall fight in the fields and in the streets, we shall fight in the hills; we shall never surrender.'

Barbed wire covered the beaches; many were mined. We were not allowed out without gas masks; black-out regulations had to be obeyed to the letter; further air-raid shelters were being erected. Moyra left her teaching job to join the Civil Defence as an ambulance driver; her father became an air-raid warden. Everyone knew Hitler's next target would be Britain, and the whole nation was preparing for heavy air attacks and a possible invasion by sea.

There was an atmosphere of excitement, dread and expectancy. 'Is this the beginning of the end?' I wondered.

The Rainfords had moved to a small seaside town half-way between Liverpool and Southport. As Dorothy had refused to return to Auntie Margery they thought that Ainsdale would be safer, and that I would be able to join them there. I did not move straight away. It was decided that I should remain where I was until the end of the summer term so that my education, such as it was, would not be disrupted more than was absolutely necessary.

By then I wasn't even sure where I wanted to live! Since my arrival in England I had really spent very little time with the Rainfords. I was very fond of them, but I was used to life at Auntie Margery's. Also, by then I had come to recognise the kindness and affection hidden beneath that rather crusty exterior.

Luckily my dilemma was solved at a stroke. Dorothy was given a new bicycle for her birthday and I, to my great delight, inherited her old one. As the two homes were not too far apart, I commuted between them. I never really moved in and I never really moved out!

I wrote about it in my diary on 18 August 1940:

Friday was my last day at school. I am really pleased I can live with the Rainfords now, but it will be terrible to say goodbye to the school and all my friends here, especially Auntie Margery. I am so used to everything, and I'll miss Jill so much. Oh, well, I'll make new friends and will try to be good. Anyway, I can come and stay here whenever I want and see all my friends, so what more could I ask for?

Something really nice happened on my last day at

school. First of all, we were given our reports and I came first in English! Then, at lunch time, Auntie Margery asked me to change into my Sunday best, and she and Moyra came back to school with me. The headmistress welcomed them and took them into the kitchen. A little later I was asked to fetch the afternoon tea and biscuits for the teachers. I went into the kitchen and had such a surprise! Lovely cakes, biscuits and sandwiches, all in my honour! The whole school had clubbed together and bought me a silver identity disc, something I have always wanted. We had such a super tea too, all thanks to dear Auntie Margery . . .

During 1940, my little world which, until then, had of necessity been almost totally English, was taking on another dimension.

The fall of France had brought many more Czechoslovak refugees to Britain. Not only were we often mentioned in the press and on the radio but, to my delight, a Czech newspaper was now being published. It was called *The Czechoslovak* and it wasn't really suitable for someone of my age but it was in CZECH and it was something to look forward to.

Olga and I corresponded regularly and whenever she could, she came to spend the weekend. She didn't join me on any hospital visits which were less frequent now anyway, as most of the Czech patients had left.

Then I learned one day that there was a whole army camp of Czech soldiers within driving distance. I nagged and pleaded until Auntie Margery finally relented and asked Uncle John to take Olga and me there. I described the trip in my diary:

We drove to North Wales, passing through the Liverpool tunnel. No one could ever guess our destination: The Czech army camp! We met a few soldiers on the way, and we shouted through the open windows to each one we passed 'Nazdar!'

Because we were Czechs the guard let us through the gate, but no English people were allowed inside. There must have been 600 tents or more, and several thousand soldiers. We couldn't stay long, we had promised Uncle John to be back soon. What a lot of 'Nazdars' there were as we walked back to the entrance!

I was near to tears. I can't say whether from joy or sorrow, but I felt so warm inside. And truly, when I meet a soldier, any soldier, I want to tell him how grateful I am, for he is fighting for my freedom too; but when I meet a Czech soldier the emotion I feel is almost too strong to bear.

A few weeks later, Olga and I tried to persuade Auntie Margery to let us go to the camp again, but this time she put her foot down. Though she was convinced that our reasons for wanting to go were quite innocent and purely patriotic, Uncle John had told her that quite a few wolf whistles had floated our way among the shouts of 'nazdar!' So, probably wisely, she decided that trips to army camps by two rather well-developed twelve-year-olds were not to be encouraged.

My parents were not forgotten; they were with me constantly. I had resigned myself to the fact that there would be no more letters. I knew I would have to be very patient and wait for the war to end. But I had faith that one day all would be well and we would be together again.

I still talked to my parents every night when I went to bed, telling them about the good things that had happened, but also about the naughty things I had done that day, promising to try and behave better. It was, in a sense, like a confessional.

After one such confession I wrote in my diary:

I know I've got to improve. I have so many faults which I must try to get rid of. Eva was quite right to tell me off. But God, it is ever so difficult. Perhaps by the time I see Eva again I won't have quite so many faults. I won't! I promise you, God, that I'll really try hard. I made the same promise to mummy and daddy and to Eva, and now

I am making it to myself. Do you hear, Vera, you've got to improve!

I was very sentimental about birthdays and other special days. One Sunday I wrote:

Today is Mother's Day – our dearest *maminka*'s day. When I think of how we celebrated last year, I am filled with longing to be back home. Oh, dearest *maminko*, this morning there is no Eva, no Vera to give you flowers and recite the poems we wrote for you. But I am sure you are looking at our photos as we are looking at yours and that you are thinking of us as we are thinking of you.

Maminko, I wish you health, happiness and contentment on your special day. May God hear our prayer for our speedy return to you so the wonderful moments we shared at home will be ours again . . .

At the start of the autumn term I was accepted as a pupil at Birkdale Central School, a step up from the council school I had been attending. At the end of a cul-de-sac, with sweeping sand dunes and the lovely Birkdale golf course almost surrounding it, the school was modern, well equipped, with friendly teachers and staff. The most important person there to me was Mr Hughes, the headmaster. He took a special interest in me, and though I was there for only a year, we became friends, and I turned to him for advice on many important matters. We remained in touch for the rest of his life.

The expected invasion of Britain never took place. The German bombers, which, after Dunkirk, concentrated on attacking British ships, airfields and aircraft factories, met with stiff opposition from RAF fighters. The attacks failed to reduce war production and not only failed to lower morale, but made the people all the more determined to win the war.

The mass raids on London and major cities later that summer were devastating, but so were the German aircraft

losses. By the middle of October it was clear that the RAF
had won the Battle of Britain. I knew and I was proud that
many Czech airmen were up there fighting with the British. I
was prouder still when afterwards Churchill said of the
fighter pilots, 'Never in the field of human conflict was so
much owed by so many to so few'.

Though out of Liverpool and danger, we were near
enough to see the enemy bombers passing overhead on their
way to the city. The air-raid warning was usually followed
almost immediately by the 'All clear' as the planes flew on
towards their target. On a clear night we could see flashes of
artillery fire in the sky, and a distant glow over the city as
incendiary bombs hit home. As Ainsdale was such a small,
insignificant town we, like most other people, hardly ever
bothered to take cover in an air-raid shelter or even under
the stairs, as we had been advised to do.

I wanted to carry on with my occasional hospital visits, but
the Rainfords did their utmost to discourage me. I argued
that Sundays were usually quiet days, and eventually
Mummy Rainford relented and allowed me to go, with
Dorothy. We were caught in an air-raid and had to run for
cover and spend several hours in a shelter, and there were to
be no more trips to Liverpool until the worst of the Blitz was
over.

Now that I was officially back with the Rainfords, my days
were fuller than ever. My new school was on the outskirts of
Southport, so when lessons were over I often cycled through
the town to spend the night and the odd weekend with
Auntie Margery. I still felt one of the family, and as Auntie
Margery had taken it upon herself to keep me supplied with
clothes, she was always in the middle of making or altering
something for me – a dress, a skirt, sometimes even a coat.

By now I had a new interest in life: boyfriends. The first
was thirteen-year-old Derek, whom I met at the Ainsdale
Sunday School. He used to take me for a walk afterwards,
sometimes followed by tea with his parents, and on special
occasions we even went to the cinema. On very special
occasions he overcame his shyness and he kissed me, but I
didn't like it much. Sixteen-year-old Vernon Farthing came

next. My name let me in for a lot of teasing. 'A diamond stoops to pick up a farthing' the children would chant. As it happened, Vernon was a public-schoolboy from a wealthy family, and he kissed better than Derek.

I liked roller-skating even better than going out with boys. I had a lovely pair of skates that Desmond had given me as a parting gift. Still my knight in shining armour, he had come to say goodbye not because I was leaving, but because he had turned eighteen and was joining the Navy.

Christmas was almost upon us, my second in England. I was to spend it with Eva, and I was looking forward to this immensely. Eva mentioned in a letter that she had written to President Benes. Not to be outdone, I decided to write too. I cannot remember exactly what I said, but I told him about my dreams, my hopes, my faith in him as our leader. Much to my delight, I received an acknowledgement of my letter, just a printed note, not even signed by him, but his own personal visiting card was enclosed.

I had been asked to sing a Czech song at a concert. I chose the Czech national anthem and borrowed Olga's national costume for the occasion. The haunting melody, the moving words of 'Where is my home?' ending with 'It is paradise on earth' brought a lump to my throat and tears to my eyes. But I was happy, for it seemed to me that by singing our national anthem and wearing our national costume I had introduced a little of Czechoslovakia to a very English audience. And on Christmas Day, shared with Eva, it was so comforting that we could whisper to one another, 'Have faith! Next year, maybe . . .'

That night I wrote in my diary:

Sometimes I think it is very wrong for us to be severed so young from our country and parents. It is lovely to get to know other people and another nation, but it would be so much better to do so knowing when we shall return home. But to be away when our country is in the hands of the Germans, when our parents may be suffering, and not knowing when we shall be able to return, that is so very very hard . . .

The winter of 1941 turned to spring and Eva joined me for the Easter holidays. She was seventeen now, and doing splendidly at school. She always loved school, and wanted to study medicine, encouraged by her English guardian. But now she was faced with a great dilemma: should she continue with her studies or leave at the end of the school year and take up nursing – and thus play her part in the fight for freedom?

The war was not going all that well. Though the RAF had won the Battle of Britain in the air, the battle on the seas was still raging. German U-boats were claiming ships and many lives; the Allied losses were appalling. Eva lived near a port; she could see the casualties that often crammed the local hospital. Now she was torn: she knew what she wanted to do, but she felt that her duty was to help the war effort. We discussed it at length, but in the end only she could decide.

It was a pleasant sunny Easter, and Eva often borrowed Dorothy's bicycle so that we could cycle into the country together. One evening we returned tired and hungry, and were very glad when we finally crawled into our beds. That night, as we lay dead to the world, we vaguely heard the familiar wail of the air-raid siren, but it was not followed by the 'All clear'. Mummy Rainford had to shake us roughly to wake us, insisting that we take shelter under the stairs.

'Don't be ridiculous,' we protested, particularly Dorothy. 'Nothing ever happens here.'

All we wanted to do was to roll over and go back to sleep, but Mummy Rainford was adamant. 'I have the strangest feeling about tonight,' she said. 'You must come downstairs.'

The five of us squeezed into the little cold cupboard and closed its door. It was very uncomfortable and very stuffy. We sat there by candlelight, like sardines. The minutes ticked by, but nothing happened. Dorothy had had enough. 'I'm going back to bed,' she announced and reached for the door. Before she had the chance to open it there was that familiar sound of a German plane overhead, followed by a new and terrifying sound of an exploding bomb, and then another, and another. The house swayed, shuddered and rumbled as if it were falling apart round us. We were blinded by dust and debris; the cupboard door had jammed, and we were trapped. We just went on sitting there, huddled together, shivering, coughing and trying to breathe – too stunned to talk.

It seemed ages before an air-raid warden released us and led us out to a waiting car which took us to a place where we were given a strong cup of tea and a bed for the night. We didn't find out what had happened until the next morning: three land-mines had been dropped on Ainsdale, probably in error. The first hit the beach and did no damage. The other two fell at either end of our street.

Miraculously, both bombs landed in soft sandy soil and sank deep into the ground before exploding. A direct hit would have wiped out the whole street and I doubt if we would have survived.

I remember walking back to our street the next morning, all of us still in our dressing-gowns. There were gaping ruins where the two corner houses had stood, yet incredibly one old lady was the only casualty. We inspected the damage to our house. There were no windows left; the walls were cracked, the roof damaged. In my room the heavy wardrobe, half the wall and most of the ceiling had fallen on the bed. How lucky for me that Mummy Rainford had for once put her foot down!

The house did not have to be demolished, but it needed substantial repairs to make it habitable again. I packed a case and returned temporarily to my other home. Auntie Margery, hearing of my narrow escape, fussed over me and gave me all my favourite foods, chief among them her scrumptious treacle pudding. I soon got over the shock and in retrospect the whole episode seemed like a scary dream.

But for the people of Liverpool, as for the people of most British cities and ports, the air attacks were a frequent terrifying reality. However, by the end of that same month, though the air attacks continued, they no longer represented the full strength of the enemy, for by then Hitler was busy making his plans to attack Russia.

In the late summer of that year I learned that a special musical performance by the Czechoslovak forces was to be held at a Liverpool theatre, and that the guest of honour was to be none other than President Benes.

Nothing could have kept me away. Luckily the Rainfords knew very well what such an occasion would mean to me and that President Benes was my hero. As by then the air-raids were not as frequent or severe, they stifled their objections, particularly when I pointed out that if it was safe enough for the president, it must be safe enough for me!

Little did I know as I left the house on the night of the performance, Benes's visiting card safely tucked in my purse, that that evening would mark a turning point in my life in England, and would, in fact, have a lasting influence on the rest of my life.

It was an unforgettable evening.

For the first time in two years I heard an accomplished male choir sing our traditional songs, I watched our national dances to the sound of well-remembered melodies, and saw men on the stage who had been fighting for our freedom – all this brought back the nostalgia, the old yearning, patriotism and pride. The emotions I felt were indescribable, particularly when I looked at the box where the president sat with his wife and the Lord Mayor of Liverpool. To share in such an occasion, to see in the flesh this man, for whose safety I prayed every night, was like a dream come true. I thought my heart would burst.

During the interval I walked up to the box; two Czech soldiers stood guard. I opened my little purse, produced the visiting card and said to one of them, 'Would you please give this to the president and tell him that Vera Diamant is waiting outside.'

The soldier was amused and surprised, but he took the card in, and a moment later returned and asked me to step inside.

President Benes greeted me, introduced me to his wife and said, 'This young lady sent me a lovely letter at Christmas.' And he actually asked me to sit with them for the rest of the performance.

'This must be a dream,' I thought, 'or am I in Heaven?'

The President wanted to hear all about my life in England and about my school. I told him how lucky I was with my English family, but not so with my education. 'I wish I could be in a proper grammar school as I would have been at home,' I said.

'You can go to one right here in England,' Benes said, with a smile. 'Here in Britain we now have a school for girls and boys like you, who are here in exile. I will give you the address, in fact I will get my own office to put in a word for you so you don't have to wait until the end of term to get in.'

I couldn't believe what I was hearing: a Czech school, here in England! A school filled with children from my own country, refugees like me. 'It will be almost like being at home,' I thought, beside myself with joy.

I drank in the rest of the president's words. 'My wife and I paid a visit to the school in July,' he continued. 'It is housed in an old manor in the heart of Shropshire. The teachers are mostly Czech too. I am sure you will like it there, for the school is like a tiny Czechoslovak colony and such a friendly place.'

Walking back from the train that night my feet barely touched the ground and I silently implored the few stars I could see to find a way to let my parents know this wonderful news, since I could no longer write to them, but wanted them to share my happiness.

Daddy Rainford, who had come to meet me, was soon infected with my excitement. He knew how desperately I longed to be among my own people and to have a better education than he could afford to provide. 'You won't be losing me, I'll be back every holiday,' I promised.

That night, for the very first time since my arrival, I fell asleep with a smile on my face, whispering as I always did, '*Maminko, tatinku*, be happy for me! I know you'll be with me tonight in my dreams.'

5

The School:
Happiness and Despair

AS SOME OF my diaries were lost in the years following the war, I have had to rely to a great extent on my memories to cover the next three years. The 1985 reunion and discussions with old friends and colleagues have done much to revive and refresh these memories.

The Czechoslovak State School in Britain was founded after the fall of France, when members of our government and forces as well as civilian families who had sought refuge in France were forced to flee again, this time to the British Isles. By the time I reached the school it had moved from its original location in Surrey to Hinton Hall, near Whitchurch in Shropshire, and had doubled in size.

There were not enough trained teachers among the civilian émigrés to staff the school which opened its doors to children of all ages between six and eighteen years, so several qualified teachers serving in the forces were seconded 'for special duty' to the school. They often taught in battle dress, and since some of the younger Czech soldiers and airmen came to the school quite regularly to sit for their matriculation examinations, the uniforms did not seem at all incongruous.

The school's aim was to provide us with a bilingual education, and to keep us in touch with our Czech culture and traditions. It also taught us to love and admire Britain; in a time of tremendous adversity for her own people, this country nevertheless had taken us in and offered us shelter and support. The school taught us that we too had an important role to play: we were, in a sense, young ambassadors from a country the world knew little about.

But on that bright autumn day in 1941 when I first saw that old, rather dilapidated building, I had no idea how much of a home it would become to me, as it did to so many of us who were separated from our parents. All I could think of, as I climbed the sweeping staircase to the front door, was that at long last my isolation from all things Czech was coming to an end.

Inside the spacious hall I was introduced to one or two members of the staff and some of my fellow-pupils. All I saw were kind and friendly faces, all I heard was Czech. I had arrived; I felt at ease and at home.

Next day I was given a test according to which I was to be assigned to a class. The teacher explained to me that the standard of Czech varied enormously from pupil to pupil. Many of the Jewish children who, like me, had fled without parents and had spent two or three years in a completely English or French environment had all but forgotten their own language, particularly the younger ones. Others who had fled from the German-speaking Sudetenland had never learned Czech properly. Here there were children of diplomats' families, sons and daughters of Czech soldiers and airmen, of political refugees, and a great number of Jewish children. There were also a few lucky children whose families had come to live in Britain well before the war to work for one of the Czech companies here. We certainly were a motley collection and it must have been a painstaking task to sort us out and ensure that each one of us achieved a reasonable academic standard.

I passed the test with flying colours – probably because I had been so very determined not to forget a single word of my mother tongue and had ensured, through keeping my diaries and reading my few Czech books over and over again, that such a calamity would never occur.

To my delight, Olga too joined the school, and was placed in my class and dormitory. It was lovely to have an old friend among so many new ones. There were two Jewish boys in my class, Honza and Seppi, who had come to England in the same transport as me. Honza had had an eventful time. On arrival he had been met by an uncle who had no means to support or accommodate him. A kind young teacher took pity on Honza and took him and a few other 'unwanted ones' to Leighton in Essex where she distributed them round various friends. Honza was to spend the night at the home of a married couple who were also teachers. These kind strangers turned their own son out of his bedroom so that Honza would have a proper bed to sleep in. That overnight stay stretched to almost a year and ended only when Honza's benefactor had to join the Navy and there was no money to spare.

He was then sent to a hostel for refugee boys near Rugby, run by a shopkeeper, Mr Overton, a truly remarkable man. As a practising Christadelphian he had striven tirelessly even prior to the occupation of Czechoslovakia to convince the British government that Jews in occupied territories were in great danger and that something must be done to save the children, first from Germany and Austria, then later Czechoslovakia. He lobbied members of Parliament and gathered a circle of supporters to form a pressure group. Many years later, when Honza visited Mr Overton, he brought down from the loft his proudest possession – a cardboard box with over two hundred labels – name tags that the children had worn round their necks when they arrived in England and came into his care; each tag represented a life that he had saved . . .

Seppi, the other 'transport child' in our form, came with his brother from Bratislava. He too had no real anchor, but had been shuffled from one foster home to another, until he came to Hinton Hall. Now he knew where he belonged. The school became his haven and home and the years spent there the happiest period of his youth.

When I told them my story, and boasted about the part President Benes played in it, Peter, another classmate, said 'He helped me too,' and went on to explain. He was one of the refugees who with his parents had first fled to France. They were a Jewish family, but his mother was German. During the fighting in France Peter and his mother had become separated from his father, who was an officer in the Czech army.

In great peril and after many hardships, Peter and his mother had managed to get on a boat to England but because of her German origins and in spite of the fact that she was fleeing from the Nazis, they were detained on arrival and held in Holloway prison. Peter was quite proud of the fact that he was the youngest Czech with a criminal record! Eventually he was transferred to a German children's home in Wandsworth. He was very Czech and he hated it there. Some kind soul gave him three pennies; he used them to buy stamps and wrote two letters: one to his mother in Holloway and the other to Benes, who intervened and had Peter transferred to the Czech school. Soon afterwards the president happened to be visiting the Czech army camp at Camberley. There, by an extraordinary quirk of fate, he was introduced to, of all people, Peter's father, who thought that his wife and son had been left behind in occupied France. 'Do you have a thirteen-year-old son?' the president asked, and when the man nodded, he said, 'Your son wrote to me', and the whole family was happily reunited as a result.

There were many stories – stories of incredible escapes, of courage and suffering. One boy, René, was barely eight years old when, with his mother, he crossed the Pyrenees on foot. They were trying to escape with a group, but a border patrol spotted them. Their guide fled, the others were killed or captured. René's mother told him to lie perfectly still and pretend to be a rock and he did, until the worst of the danger had passed. Then, hiding and creeping between the actual rocks, they eventually managed to cross the frontier.

There was the story of the two little sisters who were carried across the border in suitcases, and that of the family which crossed the frontier on a sleigh, the father, a major in the Czech army, disguised as a woodcutter. There were many sad stories too, of those who did not make it, of families separated, of relations caught and murdered. I listened with rapt attention, aware of my own uncertainty and the constant nagging question always at the back of my mind: what is happening to *my* parents? – I prayed that they were still safe and well in our home.

I was told right from the start that I would be expected to help with small everyday tasks such as tending the flower borders, darning socks and sewing buttons, and occasionally washing up, clearing the tables and preparing the vege-

tables. I didn't mind; none of us really did. In any case, I
very rarely had to peel potatoes: that chore was assigned as
punishment for naughty boys and there were enough of those
to ensure that the school never went short of peeled potatoes.

The senior girls presided over meals. Hana sat at the head
of our table. She was Jewish, three years older than me, and
despite the age difference I found her easy to talk to. One
day I confided in her that I was very worried about my sister.
She couldn't understand that at all. Why should I, a thirteen-
year-old, be worried about Eva who was seventeen and,
what is more, living in what seemed to us the lap of luxury?

'Because she's lonely,' I said simply, and this reply led to a
pen-friendship between Hana and Eva which was to last
many years. I loved my sister dearly and was very perceptive
where she was concerned. Her visit to the school the
following summer confirmed that my feelings had been
justified. She had left her school by then and had started
nursing.

Eva so loved Hinton Hall. She felt good there. I have a
letter in which she describes how she felt about that visit:

> I felt I belonged. I was with you – and I truly loved you. I was
> with people who had the same problems. We were all refugees,
> away from home in a strange land, hoping the day would come
> when we could return home.
>
> At my school and then in the hospital I was the foreigner –
> they couldn't understand my feelings even if I tried to explain. At
> Hinton Hall people just knew. I did not envy you your life, but I
> did so want to share in it, and to study. I did not at that time like
> nursing, and was not happy in my work. I was almost happy at
> your school – as much as any of us could be . . .

Eva returned to the hospital in Poole and continued with
her nursing career. Soon afterwards she was put on the
wards for the war wounded and was proud to be helping the
war effort.

At the school too we were blessed with lovely young
nurses who cared for us with unfailing affection. To us
younger ones they were almost like adopted mums with their
caring personalities. Naturally, their looks and other qual-

ities did not go unnoticed by the school's male population. It was quite remarkable how often some of the boys were sick, or in pain, so that they could enjoy, however fleetingly personal attention from one of our Florence Nightingales. There was much wailing and gnashing of teeth when one of the three engagements announced was that of the handsome maths master, the heart-throb of the senior girls.

It is hardly surprising that several marriages took place within our close-knit, in many respects isolated, community. The staff had hardly any life outside the school and were dependent on one another for company and friendship. The school was as much a home to them as it was to us pupils. We were, in a very real and important way, not so much a school as an extended family.

Though our lives were relatively self-contained, there was plenty of contact with the outside world. We frequently participated in international youth rallies, concerts and meetings. I had always loved our national dances and songs, and though no one could say I sang like a lark, I soon became a member of the school choir and dancing group. This meant that I was often among those chosen to represent my school and country; such occasions were always a welcomed interlude.

We also aroused the interest of the press and radio which gave the school a fair amount of publicity. Eventually, we even came to the attention of Buckingham Palace. One day, a barrel of honey was delivered to the school. It had been sent by the Argentine government as a gift to Princess Elizabeth and Princess Margaret. At their personal request, it was then readdressed and sent with their best wishes to the children of the Czechoslovak school. How we enjoyed those mouthfuls of royal honey after all that wartime bread and margarine!

We were lucky, for though there was a shortage of food and many items rationed or unobtainable, we had a particularly enterprising and inventive cook. It was amazing what a succulent chicken paprika she could produce with one chicken to about ten rabbits, when the luckless rabbits were careless enough to hop within the range of John Lewis's gun.

John Lewis was a farmer, and the owner of Hinton Hall. He was a well-known figure to us, for he still occupied a part of the building and was always passing by, riding his horse, or driving his horse and cart. Most of his produce had to be delivered to the Ministry of Food, but now and then there was a little surplus which usually found its way into the school's kitchen: freshly picked vegetables, a few eggs, a little extra milk or butter, and on rare occasions even a spot of cream.

Whenever our soldiers and airmen came to stay, the cook scoured the kitchen to make dishes they would dream about for weeks. We didn't mind going without our rations of butter and meat; as far as we were concerned, these men deserved the very best. But I was surprised to see the young airmen, who perhaps only a day or two earlier had faced extreme danger on bombing raids over Germany, yet remained calm and fearless, now pacing up and down, trembling at the knees, dreading the examination they had come to sit. It seemed quite incomprehensible.

I was an avid reader and spent a great deal of time in the library where these young men were often revising. It was sparsely stocked, but that we had a library at all was quite an achievement. Czech textbooks and anthologies were in particularly short supply. A few Czechs living in Britain had unearthed some outdated editions which helped a little; but it was our ingenious, hardworking staff who saved the day. Teachers turned authors and compiled their own textbooks. They even published a magazine to familiarise the very young readers with our folklore.

By comparison, we had a much more impressive selection of English books – supplied by the British Council. Eager to promote knowledge of the English language and to develop closer cultural relations, they took us under their wing, and also provided the school with English teachers. The friendly informality of the school soon melted their English reserve to the point where some even developed into real Czech chauvinists . . .

The headmaster was an army officer and a great believer in physical fitness, and he drilled us, sometimes quite mercilessly, especially the boys. It is to his credit that those who reached military age before the war ended and joined the forces, were in excellent shape. He also taught us to take in our stride such hardships as being without electricity and water, which at Hinton Hall was a common occurrence. Many times during the long winter months our taps were dry and we had to wash in the snow. I shiver at the memory of poor Hana who one freezing night was washing her hair when the flow of water stopped. She wrapped her head, full of suds, in a towel, and with a friend walked to the farmyard where there was a pump. The friend worked the pump and the water froze on Hana's head as she rinsed it.

Our generator was always breaking down, and one night this had disastrous consequences. Under cover of darkness one of the senior boys sneaked on to an upstairs balcony to have a smoke, thus breaking two rules: smoking was forbidden and the balcony was unsafe and therefore out of bounds. Suddenly there was a thunderous crash as boy and balcony plummeted to the ground. He was carried unconscious into the dining room and laid out like a corpse on one of the tables. His still body, surrounded by flickering candles, made an eerie sight. Miraculously, his only injury was a broken leg and his only punishment a severe scolding from the head. Considering the poor state of the building, it was remarkable that such accidents were the exception rather than the rule.

On Saturdays we were allowed into Whitchurch, three and a half miles away. I liked to cycle there, usually with Olga and a few of the others. The town had two important assets: a cinema and Woolworths, the only 'store' in town. The juniors, under the watchful eye of one or two teachers, were always there on Saturday mornings to spend their sixpence pocket money. I was touched to see how often they used it to buy a small gift for their mothers – those who were lucky enough to have them in England (most fathers were away in the forces).

I preferred exploring the lovely countryside surrounding Hinton Hall. There were meadows and fields, and a reasonably clean pond to swim in, and woods, which reminded me of my early childhood at home. Sometimes, as I walked through the trees I played a game of make-believe that I was still there, roaming the woods near my small town, and that my parents were waiting for me. It was now nearly three years since I had had news from them. That my anxiety was shared by so many and that my life at the school was so happy helped enormously. I loved being there so much that although I enjoyed my holidays with the Rainfords or Eva, I was soon impatient to be on the train heading back to Shropshire.

Each term our numbers grew. The teachers, one by one, had to vacate their rooms and move into lodgings to make space for additional classrooms or dormitories. Then our nearest neighbour, who lived a couple of fields away, moved out so that we could have room to expand. His manor house was large enough to house all the girls' dormitories.

It was fun walking across the fields morning and night, the cows staring silently at us with their big eyes and greeting us with a swish of their tails. But there was one sombre night when we must have resembled a funeral procession.

It was March 1943 and we older ones were listening to the nine o'clock news, as we did every night before making our way to our dormitories.

The newsreader announced, clearly and precisely, details of what was happening to Jews in Nazi concentration camps. Until that day we had all been clinging to the hope that our parents might still be at home, leading comparatively normal lives.

Maybe they were . . . Perhaps they had escaped the transports? Or were they among those doomed to die under inhuman conditions in German extermination camps? We had no way of knowing . . .

Stunned by and yet unable to absorb the full horror of what I had heard, I stumbled blindly across the dark field to my dormitory, clinging to Olga's hand. 'Whose hand will Eva cling to when she hears?' I cried inwardly.

The nightmare remained with us for endless weeks and for some of us it never went away. The teachers were now especially gentle with those of us who had to live with this new fear and uncertainty. Gloom hung over the school like a heavy cloud. Everyone was visibly shaken, everyone – Jewish or Christian – felt the tragedy, and after that life was never the same again.

That March night was the darkest of my young life. Engulfed by anguish, numbed with pain, I could neither speak nor cry. I lay there, staring into space, wishing desperately that I could take on their suffering, die for them, or at least share their fate.

Hana sat by my bed, trying to comfort me. She spent most of the night consoling those who shared my fears. Though her relatives and friends were also in peril, she felt guilty that we had to cope with such a shattering possibility while her own parents were safe in Britain.

I knew Eva was on night duty at the hospital and I doubted she would have heard the news. I poured my heart out to her in a letter the very next day. I still have her reply. She wrote in the middle of the night of 17 March 1943:

My dear little sister,

I did hear the news, and do you know, I did not cry; I dismissed it from my mind. My optimistic 'Such things are not possible' won again. But today I had your letter and I feel I must reply straight away.

How should I answer? Should I try to console, comfort and protect you? Perhaps I can help you best by telling you how I feel. I know how you hurt. I too, just like you, would gladly lay down my life for mother and father. But what would life mean to them without you and me? It would be like summer without the sun.

I still haven't shed a single tear. Not because I am so strong and brave but because so far I have had no time for myself. *Verusko,* I am now really discovering what life is all about; the path of life's discovery is hard, often very hard, but sometimes strewn with joy. I will tell you one thing I have learned: in most cases, when we grieve and weep, we are sorry for ourselves. You cry because you cannot imagine life without them. You cry at the thoughts of the hardships they *may* be suffering. Just think how much it would add to their suffering if they knew of your unhappiness! And, *Verusko,* if the very worst were to happen, isn't there time enough for grieving?

For these reasons I force myself to carry on working normally; I smile at my patients and they return my smiles and call me 'always smiling'. Thanks to Hitler, many of them are in great pain and also find it hard to smile. And they have no idea what an effort it is for me at times to give out cheerful compassion.

You can't imagine how glad I am now to be nursing. Yet tending the sick and the wounded seems such an insignificant role to play in winning the war. But every little helps.

I love our parents as much as you do, and the longer I am away from home the stronger my love for them grows. You say you cannot imagine home and a future without their presence, without their love. I too can't imagine life without them, for all our endeavours, hopes and longings are centred on us being with them. That will never change. But we shall have to live and work and be happy even if they were looking at us from Heaven. They then would be closest to us, they would watch us and over us, as we must never disappoint them. Do you understand?

I hope and believe that one day the four of us will read this letter at home. I never wanted to mention to you the possibility of our dearest ones not surviving. I did not want you to ever think of such a possibility. I ask you again: live, be happy, don't grieve. You say that everything you do is for *them,* so be happy for *them.* Have faith and be patient – TRUTH WILL PREVAIL!

I read Eva's letter many times. It helped not only me, but many of my friends who had no kind big sister to turn to. I could see the logic of her reasoning. Determined to follow Eva's advice and example, I locked my anxiety deep within and threw myself into my studies and the school's activities.

Some time later in 1943, Eva received a brief note from an acquaintance of father's which said that both our parents had been taken from their home and interned in the ghetto of Terezin. After the initial shock, Eva wrote to me in her gentle optimistic way: 'Don't be sad, believe that all will be well'.

My dear big sister! She shared my anxieties and longings, and she herself had no one to lean on. Yet her first concern was always how I would react to any sad news, and she always tried to soften the blows.

I knew Terezin only as the town where our train had stopped for several hours on the way to England, while we waited for some important documents to catch up with us. I had paid no attention to the place then – how could I have known that it would loom so large in the lives of our family?

We made enquiries through the Red Cross and found that they were well informed about this very old fortress town. It had been cleared of its Aryan population and was now entirely Jewish. A German propaganda film had been made about the life in Terezin, which was shown throughout Germany and then distributed to Britain and the Allies to prove to the world just how decently Hitler was in fact treating the Jews and to show that the horrific tales of extermination camps were just grossly exaggerated rumours.

The film, *Hitler Makes the Jews the Present of a Town,* showed that within the ghetto walls Jews transported there from Bohemia and Moravia, and later from other parts of Europe, were leading comparatively normal, though very restricted, lives. The overcrowding was appalling, food and fuel were scarce, but such were the hardships of war . . . They were certainly not being massacred. Far from it: the town was self-governing; Jewish men and women ran shops and offices; Jewish doctors and nurses worked in the hospitals; children attended school. There were synagogues and there were theatres in which plays, operas and concerts were performed by well-known Jewish artists. A handful of Jews were even allowed to board a train sent by the Swiss Red Cross to carry them to freedom . . .

The free world preferred to believe what it saw on the film rather than the harrowing reports brought out by the very few who managed to escape the concentration camps and make their way into unoccupied territory. 'They must be exaggerating – it can't be that bad' was most people's reaction. How could one blame them? Didn't my own sister say 'Such things are not possible'?

So how was a mere child to guess that the object of the film was to blind the world to the truth, that the old town of

Celakovice, summer 1939:
ever-faithful Marta and my kittens

Dressed in national costume for a Christmas concert in 1940, I sang the Czech national anthem 'Where is my Home?'

Dorothy's thank-you photograph for my parents, who sent the skirt and jacket

Eva doing her best for the war effort, summer 1944

Hinton Hall, our school's stately but crumbling home, and its motley inhabitants in 1942. Can you spot me? I'm the busty one wearing a jacket

Terezin was, in fact, primarily used as a gathering and staging post where the Jews were collected and then, after shorter or longer stays, sent to their final destination. They were told, and some believed, that they were going to labour camps where conditions would be better.

Life in Terezin was a far cry from what the film presented: there was little work, people were dying of cold, hunger and disease, yet here at least they had a chance to survive, particularly those of mixed marriages who rarely moved on. All the others, thousand upon thousand, travelled on, their trains taking them not to the labour camps they had been led to expect, but to the gas chambers of Auschwitz and other concentration camps.

The German propaganda film did not show the so-called 'Little Fortress' on the outskirts of Terezin which had been turned into one of the most dreaded Gestapo prisons. In its dungeons prisoners were subjected to such bestial treatment and torture that very few came out alive.

Thank God, I did not know then that a collaborator in our little town of Celakovice had reported to the Gestapo that my father, instead of handing over his business to the Germans, as all Jews had been ordered to do, had made a private deal with an Aryan friend who had nominally taken the business over, and that both this man and my own dear father were now being held and tortured in that notorious prison . . .

6
Our Welsh Haven

BY 1943 HINTON Hall was bursting at the seams again and literally crumbling about our ears. Packed as it was to the rafters, the building now had so many 'unsafe' areas that it was impossible for the staff to cope and more space was desperately needed.

Then one day at lunchtime the dining room ceiling came crashing down. Luckily most of us had finished our meal and were standing by the window watching farmer John galloping by on his horse. The ceiling collapsed immediately above where many of us had just been sitting. Miraculously, no one was hurt, except little René who had a broken finger.

This brush with disaster made the headmaster even more determined to have the school transferred to new premises. Eventually the primary school moved to Maesfen Hall near Nantwich and alternative premises were also allocated for the secondary school. We were to be housed in a hotel built shortly before the outbreak of war, taking it over from Bromsgrove Public School which was returning to Birmingham.

I shall never forget our arrival in the village of Llanwrtyd Wells, a small community which lies at the very heart of central Wales. We spilled out of the steam train at the tiny station and marched with our bags and cases along an unmade road. We could hardly believe our eyes when we saw our new home, for we had acquired not only a spacious modern building, but also several acres of rolling pastures, complete with cows, a pretty boating lake and a stretch of the fast-flowing river Irfon for our playground.

Needless to say, the arrival of so many Czech youngsters (there were about 130 of us by then) caused quite a stir in the village and at first we were viewed with a mixture of curiosity and suspicion. Then one of our teachers had a brainwave: we organised a concert, to which all the people of Llanwrtyd Wells were invited, and most of them came! The audience loved our national songs and dances, and when at the end all the pupils of the school stood up and sang the Welsh national anthem *in Welsh* there was not a dry eye in the house. Our new Welsh friends, for friends they became there and then, opened their homes and their hearts to us all.

After our move to Wales a new English teacher joined the staff; her predecessor had been a rather prim and humourless spinster who was none too popular. But now she was gone and instead there was Miss Mackenzie, 'on loan' from the British Council, of course. She arrived as a very raw and wide-eyed recruit straight from college, and looked positively alarmed when she found herself among so many strange foreigners. But in no time at all she won us all over, teachers and pupils alike, with her vibrant Scottish voice, her beaming smile and genuine warmth.

Her presence at the school brought a welcome addition to my school programme. Miss Mac, as we fondly called her, was keen on sport, especially hockey, and she decided to turn one of the meadows into a hockey field and to introduce us girls to the sport.

She charmed the British Council into sending us hockey sticks and other necessary equipment while we busied ourselves marking out the hockey field.

I was good at sport and was elected captain of the team, a post I proudly held until my years at the school came to an end. Miss Mac was our coach and keenest supporter, and I in turn one of her greatest fans. Apart from enjoyment and exercise, this sport brought closer contact with several Welsh schools in the county, which resulted in many new friendships.

As our numbers grew, I was not surprised to see two newcomers, both Jewish, in my class. Harry, a tall and lanky boy, was one of them. He informed us, almost casually, that he was so keen to join us that he actually ran away from his English boarding-school. I was most impressed until he spoilt it all by adding, 'I spent two weeks at the Hinton Hall summer camp. I liked the atmosphere, and I liked the food even better. I made up my mind there and then to join this school; the food at my other school was terrible . . .'

Harry had come to England in January 1939 in one of the very first children's transports, organised by the Barbican Mission whose aim was to convert the young Jewish refugees to Christianity. Most of the forty or fifty Czech children who were with Harry at the Chislehurst home in Kent, run by the Mission, had already been baptised in Prague; that was the condition of acceptance. Harry was one of the few exceptions. Nevertheless, during his short stay at the home he became quite involved in the church and religious instruction, and enjoyed being a choirboy. He was fortunate; his parents and young sister, who had stayed behind in Prague, managed to get away from the Nazis, helped by a friend of Harry's father, a prominent German lawyer who lived in Prague. Shortly after Harry's departure, this man handed his father an envelope and said, 'I have some influence with the German authorities. Should you and your family need to follow your son to England, take this letter to headquarters. This is my personal authorisation of your visas.'

The Germans marched into Prague on 15 March 1939 and on that same day Harry's father, armed with letter and passports went to their headquarters. To his immense relief, the visas were duly stamped – numbers one and two – the very first to be issued under Nazi rule. He hurriedly instructed his wife by telephone to meet him immediately at the station; she left home with their little daughter, carrying only a shopping bag, so as to avoid attracting attention.

Thus, to Harry's delight, the family was reunited. Like so many others, they came empty-handed and had to start rebuilding their lives, but they were all safe.

At least five children from the Chislehurst home made their way to our school, and held on to their Jewish faith. But of those who remained in the care of the Barbican Mission several became ordained as ministers of the church. The most remarkable story is that of twin brothers, Joseph and Peter Schneider, who at the age of ten fled with Harry to Britain. Their parents died in the holocaust and they remained in the care of the Barbican Mission after the war. Joseph studied medicine and went to work as a medical

missionary in Africa; as far as I know he is still there. Peter
entered the church, and was first chaplain of a college at
Cambridge University, then of a church in Haifa, and later
canon of the Anglican cathedral in Jerusalem. By the time
he moved back to England his knowlege of Hebrew and
Jewish religion was so extensive that he would have put
many a modern rabbi to shame. But then Peter never
disclaimed his Jewish background; all his life he felt as much
a Jew as a Christian.

Harry had neither seen nor heard of Peter since the early
days of the war. They met again by a remarkable coinci-
dence. A few years ago we were both invited to friends in
Burpham, a small Sussex village. 'You must meet our vicar,'
said our hostess, 'he is a countryman of yours.'

Upon hearing the name 'Peter Schneider' Harry exclaimed, 'Not only will I be delighted to meet him, but I'll be
delighted to meet him *again*!'

Thus, after more than forty years, two men who had last
seen each other as eleven-year-olds sat at the same table,
and over dinner an old friendship was re-established. Harry,
being a dentist, promised to do his best to save Peter's teeth
if he in turn would try to save his soul . . .

As well as being the vicar of Burpham, Peter was an
adviser to the Archbishop of Canterbury on inter-faith
matters. As the archbishop's envoy he travelled extensively,
particularly to Israel, and worked tirelessly to bring about
greater understanding and unity.

The high esteem in which he was held by the theological
community was reflected in the memorial service held in
Westminster Abbey after his untimely death. The
Archbishop of York and the Archbishop of Canterbury both
officiated; the lesson from the Old Testament was read by
Hugo Gryn, a London rabbi of Czech origin. Christians,
Jews and Moslems of many nationalities sat side by side at
this thanksgiving service for the life and work of Peter
Schneider, Christian by religion, Jewish by birth, who had
come to these shores as a small Czech refugee boy . . .

I suspect Peter's life would have turned out very different-
ly had he chosen to join the Czech school . . .

Many of my fellow-students had parents in Britain, so naturally certain weekends were earmarked for their visits to the school. On such occasions the staff discreetly organised activities for those of us on our own, so that we wouldn't feel left out. Nevertheless, on visiting days I always felt miserable, homesick and very envious. Sometimes I fantasised that my parents had boarded a train in Terezin bound for freedom, and suddenly appeared, running towards me . . .

Although Mummy Rainford would have liked to come and see me often, she came only once, and then not on a visiting day. At that time there was so little money to spare, and she preferred to concentrate on the holidays when the whole family spoiled me terribly. They knew that at the school I was in excellent hands and that my welfare was being more than adequately catered for by the Czech government.

But I longed for a visitor, any visitor, a relative, any relative to come and brighten that special day for me. So I was delighted when thanks to Jula – the other new boy in my class – I discovered an uncle in England. He was my mother's cousin, once or twice removed, but when relatives are scarce, any, however distant, are better than none.

Uncle Pavel was living in the Lake District where he met and befriended Jula – another 'transport boy'. When he learned of my existence he decided to visit us both. I was so excited and proud when, dressed in my Sunday best, I walked with Jula to have lunch with Uncle Pavel at the local hotel. I learned that he had managed to get out of Czechoslovakia with a little capital, which he used to purchase a few second-hand machine tools. He set them up in a terraced house, hired a few local girls, and by 1941 was producing components for, among others, Rolls Royce aircraft engines.

As he worked long hours, and seven days a week, he came only that once, but we remained in touch and his visit boosted my morale and made me feel less alone.

Rather than join in the organised activities, whenever other pupils' parents were about, I preferred to go for long cycle rides with Olga, Alice and Margit, who shared my sentiments about visiting days. More often than not, our destination was an isolated farm up in the Brecon hills where the elderly owners always welcomed us with a cup of tea, home-made scones and sometimes, as a special treat, fresh boiled eggs. The mothers of our more fortunate schoolmates ensured that they never went short of home-made cakes, biscuits and sweets, so our Welsh friends' hospitality helped to make us feel less neglected and sorry for ourselves.

One day we had a very pleasant surprise. A parcel arrived from an anonymous donor, addressed to the four of us, and we opened it to find a whole roast chicken and some fresh fruit. We strolled through the school grounds eating the delicious chicken and tossing the bones over our shoulder as we had seen Charles Laughton do it as Henry VIII. No chicken before or since has ever tasted so good. We found out some time later that our mysterious benefactor was the headmaster's odd-job man, who had very little contact with pupils. This thoughtful generous gesture from a near-stranger meant so much to us. The thought of it still warms me today.

I would have been equally thrilled if some anonymous benefactor had sent me a parcel containing one particular practical item – a real brassière. Mummy Rainford, bless her, had no idea what to do with a busty fifteen-year-old and as I was still a child in her eyes, she thought that my bosom should be concealed or at least camouflaged. So, instead of providing me with a proper support bra she bought me a very old-fashioned 'liberty bodice' – a misnomer if ever there was one. Thick elastic at the back with a wide shapeless panel of heavy satin in front, it was like a strait-jacket which did nothing to enhance the figure and made me look and feel as if encased in a barrel!

1943 was a very eventful year – for me, the school, but, above all, for the course of the war. Before 1943 the Allies had suffered many defeats. Then, at last, victory at Alamein, followed by victory at Stalingrad, marked the turning point of the war, and from then on the Allies advanced steadily. There was no doubt in anyone's mind that the war would soon be over, and that it would end in victory. But there was still a long way to go.

We followed the progress of the war most avidly in the press and on the radio, and had our own daily news bulletin, compiled by Seppi. He rose at dawn to monitor the BBC news relayed to Merchant Navy ships at sea, decode it and type it out. The end product was then nailed to a bulletin board for everyone to read when they came down to breakfast. This was the modest beginning of Seppi's distinguished career in journalism.

The members of our government and forces took a keen interest in the school and from time to time came to give us talks on developments in the war. These were exciting days, and our return to our own free country no longer seemed such a distant dream. Yet, wrapped in the safety of the peaceful Welsh hills the fighting seemed far removed from our lives.

Then, early one evening, as we were preparing for the school monthly dance, we heard a plane overhead. This was nothing unusual as there was an American base nearby, but this plane was flying too low and the engine didn't sound right. We ran out, heard an explosion, then saw a flash and thick smoke rising. We all started running towards the plane, but the headmaster turned us back, allowing only the senior boys and the teachers to accompany him. They returned several hours later, pale and shaken. A twin engined Wellington bomber had crashed; there were no survivors. The boys had helped to transport the bodies to the local chapel which was turned into a mortuary. 'The most eerie thing,' said one of them, 'was that their watches were still ticking . . .'

The help given by the school in dealing with this disaster brought us even closer to the people of Llanwrtyd Wells. Most of the able-bodied men of the village had been called up, but of those who remained several were connected with the school, some as part-time teachers. There were local women among the nurses and domestic personnel; village boys marched and drilled with our Air Training Corps contingent. Our Boy Scouts troup often joined in the activities of the Llanwrtyd Scouts. As a matter of fact the only non-Welsh Scouts entitled to wear the Dragon of Wales on their uniforms are the Scouts of our school . . .

Because of our ever-increasing numbers, a few of the teachers moved into lodgings in the village. There was an atmosphere of genuine friendliness and mutual acceptance between the two communities which made us feel very much at home.

There was one man in particular – Jim Jones was his name – who was a friend to us all. He had a little corner shop and an old minibus into which he somehow squeezed a whole football team or a hockey team whenever we needed transport. He took us not only to matches but on many outings, and supplied the younger children with sweets and the older ones with forbidden unobtainable luxuries such as cider and cigarettes.

When Harry and I called on Jim in the summer of 1978, he was an invalid living alone. He had fond memories of those years when he was so involved in our lives; he even remembered pupils' names, regretting only that just a handful had wandered back over the years to see the old place and to pay him a visit. He reminisced about one boy in particular, Bobby, once the star of our football team and school plays, who had in later life become a millionaire. 'Ask him to send me a cigar,' Jim said jokingly, and this we did, and Bobby sent him a box of the very best.

It is no wonder that Bobby has made such a success of his life. Even as a boy he was almost unfairly blessed with brains, charm, looks and eloquence. Singing, dancing and acting were just a few of his other talents. He invariably played the hero in both the Czech and English plays we put on, usually with me as his leading lady, for much to my delight I had discovered a flair for acting.

Life seemed exceptionally full during those last two years of the war, with a busy school programme combined with

outside activities. One memorable week in 1943 Bobby and I
and a few others represented our school and country at an
International Youth Rally in Edinburgh. This was my first
visit to Scotland, and I fell in love with the lovely city not
least because Prince's Street somehow reminded me of Saint
Wenceslas Square in Prague. 'It won't be long now, it can't
be long before I am walking down my favourite Prague
street again,' I promised myself. Such rallies now generated
a tremendous feeling of expectancy, hope and eagerness for
the day when we could start building a better world in our
own countries.

I was fifteen when I fell in love for the first time. His name
was Walter, and he was a latecomer to the school who said
very little about his past; I did not question him, knowing
instinctively that he did not wish to talk about it. All I knew
was that he wasn't Jewish and that his parents were political
refugees who had fled from Sudetenland, which accounted
for his Czech being so poor.

He was the first boy who made me realise that there was
more to a boy-girl relationship than holding hands and an
occasional peck on the cheek. He was the first boy who
aroused my feelings, made me aware of my femininity and
made me feel desirable, almost beautiful. I felt strangely
guilty for loving him because all the love in my heart should
have belonged to mother and father. Yet even then I knew
that this was a different kind of love, one which did not
interfere with my feelings for them, and it gave me
something else to think and dream about.

Ours was such a pure innocent relationship, but it opened
the door to a mysterious unexplored new world. I enjoyed
our 'romance' – the walks along Lovers Lane, boating on the
lake, swimming in the river, dancing together at the school
dances, and Walter was such a fine dancer too! More than
anything, I marvelled at the strange emotions ignited by a
mere glance, touch of the hand or a kiss.

Sometimes I wondered why I had not fallen for someone
with a similar background and more in common with me,

but then such boys were like brothers to me, and Walter's main attraction was in being different.

Much to my sorrow, Walter's stay at the school was brief, because he couldn't master the Czech language. He left at the end of 1944 and started work in Liverpool. I consoled myself with the thought that I'd be able to see him during the holidays, and that we could write. I knew he cared about me too. What I didn't know was that he was consumed with shame and guilt because of his German origins. Knowing that my parents were suffering internment or worse, he felt he had no right to my affection and that I would despise him when I found out the truth. That was why he did his best to break with me once he had left school, which at the time baffled and upset me.

Once again I can turn to my diaries which cover in great detail the happenings and the sentiments of the last few months of the war, and beyond.

Everyone felt that 1945 would see the end of the war and there was an air of excitement throughout the school. The Allies were advancing, the Germans retreating – yet in spite of the defeat which loomed before them, they did not stop their mass extermination of the Jews; if anything, it gathered momentum. By then the Allied leaders could no longer ignore the evidence of what Hitler's 'Final Solution' really meant. Too many authentic, often documented accounts of what was happening to Jews, particularly at Auschwitz, the biggest extermination camp, had reached the free world. Even then the full extent of the horror was not known.

For those of us waiting impatiently for news, excitement and anticipation alternated with doubt and fear. I clung to the hope that my parents were still in the 'model camp' Terezin, though we had not received a word from or of them during the past three years. At the beginning of 1945 I started a new diary, and in my first entry I wrote:

This book is the ninth of my diary, and I firmly believe that before I fill its pages victory will be ours. Mother . . .

father . . . I think of you constantly. If only we had some news! It has been such an endless anxious wait. I pray so hard that you will be spared.

Now that my return home was almost a reality instead of a dream, I was suddenly insecure and plagued with doubt. One moment I would be happy, the next gripped by fear. What if they had not survived? How would I cope with life in Czechoslovakia without them? How could I even face it? How much simpler and easier it would be not to return, to make my life with the Rainfords or accept Auntie Margery's sincere and generous offer to adopt me.

My determination – my faith in myself – had momentarily, and understandably, faltered. I turned for guidance to Mr Hughes, the headmaster of Birkdale Central School where I had spent a brief but happy year. He befriended me then and we had remained friends, and I knew his advice would be sound, sincere and unemotional. I still have the beautiful letter he sent in reply:

13th February 1945

My dear Vera,

You will be surprised at getting such a quick reply to your letter which I only received this morning, but I felt you were unhappy, full of doubts as to the future and not sure which way duty lies.

Well, first of all let us see what you have done. While here you were very popular with scholars and teachers, and made remarkable progress. What does this mean to Czechoslovakia? In the minds of your friends you represent your country and when the name is mentioned a friendliness for your people is the thought that enters the minds of all you have associated with. In this way you have been a little ambassador of good will between Britain and your country.

What of the future? Of course you would like to stay in England, and England would welcome such as you, but you have a duty to your country, to your people.

First of all you can speak with authority about the people of Britain. You say you feel half English. You can foster a friendship between the two countries. With your brain you can help in the reconstruction of a country that I have always admired.

I do hope that your parents will come through all right and that you will be united once again. After their suffering they will be changed, perhaps broken in spirit or in health. There again your bright joyous and loving nature will help to heal their wounds.

I send to you again our war motto: 'Be of good cheer.'

Do you know the poem by Arthur Hugh Clough, 'Fight on'? Read it and teach it to your people. I have found it a great help. The Prime Minister quoted a portion of it in one of his speeches.

Don't hesitate to write to me at any time, about anything. I have never been a headmaster to my scholars. I think perhaps father would be the better word.

God bless you little girl. Fight on.

Yours very sincerely, R.H. Hughes

And on a separate sheet, in his own hand, he wrote the poem out for me:

Fight On   Arthur Hugh Clough
Say not the struggle nought availeth,
The labour and the wounds are vain,
The enemy faints not, nor faileth,
And as things have been, things remain.

If hopes were dupes, fears may be liars,
It may be in yon smoke concealed,
Your comrades chose e'en now the fliers,
And but for you possess the field.

For while the tired waves vainly breaking,
Seen here no patient inch to gain,
Far back through creeks and inlets making,
Comes silent, flooding in, the main.

And not by eastern windows only,
When daylight comes, comes in the light,
In front the sun comes slow, how slowly,
But westward, look, the land is bright.

Mr Hughes's letter helped me to make up my mind once and for all: I would return home, come what may. I settled down to my studies and worked harder than ever, determined to take back the best possible report. Now and then I thought of Walter. I was upset that I had not heard from him for more than a month. On 18 February I wrote in my diary:

> There was a dance last night; we had something to celebrate. This afternoon our football team beat Llandridnod 8:1, and everyone was in a good mood. But how I missed dancing cheek to cheek with Walter! He is such a lovely dancer, so gentle and attentive. The music brought back many memories. I danced non-stop, mainly with Harry, and sometimes I closed my eyes and pretended he was Walter . . .
> Why doesn't he write? Is this the end? I feel so let down by his silence. I want to know what is going on! I was so sure he liked me a lot. Surely he couldn't forget me so quickly.

But I didn't have much time to fret and worry about Walter. The hockey season was in full swing, and as captain I was much involved in all the planning and training. Our team competed in the county championship. We didn't win it, of course, but we held our own. After lengthy descriptions of all the matches, I wrote:

> We had lunch in Brecon County School. It really is a lovely school. We ate with about two hundred girls, a few teachers and some Lords and Sirs; I am not sure why they were there. The food wasn't bad but there was too little of it: a single potato, a mouthful of carrot and a few bits of meat followed by an enormous sponge pudding which didn't go far when cut into twenty portions. Luckily our school's cook had supplied us with sandwiches, so we didn't go hungry.

Later that same week I made a very different entry:

> Last Thursday the list of Jews who have been taken from Terezin to Switzerland arrived at the school. I hoped so very much as I scanned the list that mother's and father's

names would be on it, but they weren't. I would be lying if I said that I wasn't bitterly disappointed, but I am getting used to such blows and to taking them without tears. I can only hope and pray that they will survive and that we shall all be together again, and soon.

That night I couldn't fall asleep. From my bed I gazed at the sky, and through the branches of the trees I could see just one lonely star. I thought again of mother's words, 'Let the sun and the stars be the messengers of our love and our thoughts' and as I watched the little star and thought of mother, she seemed so very near.

'Fly to her, little star, tell her I think of her constantly; give her my love and kisses; tell her that maybe soon we shan't be needing you to be our messenger, that we shall be able to say what is in our hearts to each other in person.'

All at once the star was gone. I craned my neck to see it, but it had disappeared. I fell asleep happy, warmed by the childish, yet comforting thought that the little star was on its way to fulfil its mission.

There was something else just then which occupied my mind and time. I had been chosen to play Katharina, with Bobby as Petruchio, in Shakespeare's *The Taming of the Shrew*. This demanding role marked the peak of my acting career at the school; the performance was to take place before Easter.

But I was in for an unpleasant surprise:

Man proposes – God disposes. I expected a great end of term, full of excitement and fun, but here I am lying up here in the sick-bay while all the others are enjoying themselves. But I mustn't complain, for it was all my own fault.

Last week was so exhausting, what with the end of term exams, rehearsals, hockey practice, re-marking the field. I got precious little sleep, but I was in great spirits. Saturday was the big night. We had the dress rehearsal in the morning; we were all nervous, including me. Miss Mac

told me to rest afterwards, but I said the sun and the fresh
air would do me good, and went out for a walk. Some of
my friends were playing volleyball and I just couldn't
resist, I had to join in. The good Lord punished me then: I
tripped and fell, and something cracked in my right foot. I
hopped up and down and cried out with the pain. Olga
and Alice almost carried me to the surgery where I
whispered 'water, water' and then passed out. When I
came to a few minutes later, I was lying on a bench; there
was a compress on my foot and someone was pouring
water down my shirt instead of into my mouth. 'Serves me
right' I kept repeating to myself. 'But what about next
week's return match with Brecon and, oh crikey! what
about tonight's performance?'

It was the doctor's afternoon off, so someone was sent
into the village to find him and I was left alone with my
own gloomy thoughts. But I had to chuckle when I heard
remarks like 'No performance tonight, the shrew's already
been tamed' floating through the window. I thought I
must have sprained my ankle, but within minutes there
were shouts of 'Have you heard the latest? Vera's broken
her ankle.' Someone actually said I had broken my
leg . . .

Nevertheless, it was no joke. I didn't have an
understudy, and everyone was looking forward to the
performance. I kept my fingers crossed that the doctor
would let me play and I wouldn't let them all down.

As news of my accident spread, teachers and friends
appeared in the sick-bay. Most of the boys were at
football training, but the moment they returned the whole
team burst through the door, Bobby in the lead. 'You
can't do this! You've got to go on! You will be able to,
won't you?. . .' Bobby stayed with me to see the doctor
who, seeing our anxious faces, and probably against his
better judgement said he would allow me to go on as long
as I promised to be careful. He bound my foot tightly with
elastoplast, and Bobby patiently taught me how to walk.
Before the performance, when the names of the cast were
read and my name was called, everyone clapped and

shouted 'hurrah!' Thus encouraged I acted as best as I
could – the wild Katharina hobbling through her scenes –
and perhaps, because of the challenge, I gave the best
performance ever.

This was great for my morale but bad for my ankle.
Back in the sickroom my whole foot started throbbing so
badly that I was moaning with pain; this brought Miss Mac
to my bedside. When an aspirin failed to do the trick, she
sat up with me the whole night, and in the morning had
me carried to the doctor's surgery.

I was hoping that he would take off the elastoplast
and tell me to run along and be more careful next time,
but my foot looked so bruised and swollen that he
hesitated even to let me go away for Easter! Eventually he
wrapped my foot in cotton wool, then in the hated
elastoplast, and ordered me to spend my holiday lying or
sitting down with no walking at all. What a bore! I had so
many things planned – but what could I do?

Alice helped me to pack and Miss Mac lent me her
walking stick and a huge slipper because nothing else
fitted my foot. She also made me take £2 to buy myself a
new pair of shoes. The day we broke up I was loaded with
everyone's luggage into the lorry and taken to the station.
I couldn't walk at all and quite honestly the thought of the
long journey with several changes scared me. But my
friends turned into guardian angels who watched over me
and my luggage and almost carried me from platform to
platform. This slowed us down, I missed my connection in
Crewe and had to wait two hours. From there I was
travelling alone.

Mummy Rainford always met me in Liverpool, but, to
my horror, this time when I really needed her, she wasn't
there. I must have looked a very sorry sight standing on
the empty platform next to my case, shod in Miss Mac's
large slipper, leaning on the stick, sniffing hard to keep
the tears at bay. A porter passed by, pulling a luggage
cart. Seeing my stricken face and the sorry state I was in,
he asked jokingly, 'Which front have you come from?' but
he took pity on me and said, 'Come on lass, sit yourself

here, I'll take you to wherever you want to go.' So I rode
in style on the luggage cart to the taxi rank where a
solitary taxi happened to be waiting; it took me to the
other station where, with the taximan's help I was put on a
train to Ainsdale. Here my luck caught up with me again,
for Dorothy, on her way from work, caught the same
train. I sighed with relief and left everything else to her.

The Rainfords had planned to take me to my very first
ball. I was going to go skating, swimming and cycling and to
visit friends. But instead of that I had to behave like an
invalid. On 4 April I made a long entry in my diary:

I've received so many letters! Knowing that this silly foot
of mine is stopping me from doing things, friends keep
writing to cheer me up. But I haven't heard from Walter.
It just doesn't make sense . . . I am really sorry not to
have seen him this holiday. He could have brightened
these rather boring days. I often think how nice it would
be if he turned up. I even dreamed about him once. But I
shouldn't really think of him at all.
   My ankle is improving slowly, in fact now I can hop
around the house on both feet and even help a little. I've
been knitting like mad. I seem to be gripped by a knitting
fever. I've made socks for Daddy Rainford, a pair for
myself and some gloves too, all without a pattern, straight
from my head. I never thought I would inherit this
particular skill from mother, but I am very pleased that I
have. At least it helps to pass the time.
   Last Friday Mummy Rainford brought home the most
hideous contraption. In England they call it a bath chair; I
have no idea what it is in Czech. It's quite comfortable, I
must admit, and it helps to get me about, but I hate it!
Everyone looks at me pityingly, as if to say 'You poor
little mite' and I feel like leaping up and shouting 'Save
your pity, I'm not really an invalid! It's only a sprained
ankle!' Mummy Rainford had borrowed this monstrosity
from the church. On Friday they pushed me all the way to
Shirley Hill, and that is four miles away, to hear a sermon

and have tea. The tea was very good and the sermon
passable, but all that talk made my head ache; I nearly
froze to death on the way home. On Sunday they pushed
me again, this time to church. I vowed that I'd never ride
in that bath chair again. I am determined to get to
Southport without it at least once to see a good film, and
am keeping my fingers crossed that my ankle will behave.

Now I want to turn to the most important day of the
week, last Saturday, mother's birthday. 'Oh, *maminko*, I
thought of you so many times! Are you alive? Are you
well? I couldn't send you even the briefest greeting, I
could only pray for you, and father too. If you are alive, if
you know what is happening in the world then you need
no gift or greetings, for our dearest wish should come true
very soon, the wish I cried out so impulsively as the train
was leaving Prague: 'See you again in a free
Czechoslovakia!' Do you remember? – What a lot has
happened since that day! You and father must have been
through so much since we said goodbye. I often tremble
with fear when I think of it, and hope and pray that you
have been spared and that one day soon we shall be able
to prove to you that we have not forgotten for a single
moment that we are your daughters and daughters of
Czechoslovakia.

Maminko, so much is happening! The Allies have
crossed the Rhine and are advancing through Germany
and Holland. The Russians have already freed Vienna and
are now fighting in Slovakia. The Germans are fleeing on
all fronts, or giving themselves up to the Allied forces.
They know they cannot escape defeat, so they are trying
at least to get away with their bare lives. I feel some pity
for them, but also an overpowering bitterness and hate.
They caused the destruction of Europe, they committed
mass murder and the vilest brutalities. They have fully
earned their dishonour and disgrace, they deserve
everything that is coming to them now . . .

Maminko, you so love the spring, you say it is the most
beautiful season – and now it has begun. Can you see and
feel it, can you rejoice with it? Can you see the world

slowly awakening and rising to its feet, can you see with the first signs of spring the first signs of hope, peace and freedom? It won't be long before Europe, like the buds on plants and trees, will burst into flower again, and at last the world will be able to rejoice. The end is coming. The dawn is breaking. The storm is dying . . . I can barely hear it in the distance. The birds are singing, the sun is shining, everything is in bloom. Spring is here, your favourite time of the year. Smile at the sun, draw joy and strength from its rays. The whole world is awakening . . .

Yesterday I brought out yours and father's letters; they are my greatest treasure. I reread them all, and drew comfort from the words. Some I translated for Mummy Rainford and Dorothy, delivering your messages and wishes which in my pigeon-English of a few years ago must have sounded very clumsy. I am staggered to find how much I have grown up since then. Fancy asking for doll's clothes and childish things like that when I knew how difficult it was to send anything at all. But you would have done anything to please me. Father often joked and didn't hesitate to scold me. But deep love and concern for our happiness flows through every line . . . 'Believe that we are happy and that we have faith . . . We know you shall always make us proud and that you will never let us down . . . You are our treasure, our sun, our all . . .'

Tatinku, do you realise that I am a year older than Eva was when we came to England? What will you think of me? Will you be proud of me? I have grown in character as well as size; my willpower has hardened and faith, hope and love have anchored firmly in my heart. I love you both so much. I want to fly to you right now . . . I must be patient.

I am determined to stay happy and to work hard. I am so grateful to my school. It is giving me an education such as the Rainfords couldn't afford and is helping me not to be a burden to them. And I am so happy there. It is like home and therefore like Heaven – except that you are missing and so terribly missed. I am crying, because I so long for your love, for your embrace, for the family life we

shared. I am so afraid. Will God listen? Has he heard my
constant prayer? –

Believe this: if, God forbid, you should not be waiting
for us, I shall try to live as you would have wanted me to –
and I would still live for you. For you and your great
sacrifice, for your love and your unfulfilled dreams.
Tatinku, maminko, that is my promise.

I am looking at your photograph and at the picture of
Celakovice. They are set in a cardboard folder which Eva
made me for our first Christmas here. On the front page
she drew a bunch of flowers tied with ribbons in our
national colours, with the motto 'Truth will prevail'
underneath. Inside the folder there is a picture-postcard
of our town and above it the inscription 'HOME'. On the
opposite side two love birds are singing the words 'I
BELIEVE', and beneath them is the last photograph of you
two.

I am not going to lose you, am I? We'll read these lines
together, won't we, and laugh together at my worries.
Good night, my dearest ones. God bless you both.

7

Where Were You, God?

THREE DAYS LATER I was back at school. My ankle was almost as good as new, and I threw myself into the well-known routine, happy to be busy, happy to be back with my friends, without too much time for thought. The weather was fine, the news was good. By the end of April the Allies were in Berlin. And then Brno in Moravia was freed by the Red Army. I was so thrilled and proud to hear the Czechoslovak national anthem played on the radio. 'Bohemia will be next,' I promised myself, 'and then my parents will be freed . . .' I felt so strange as I listened. There was a lump in my throat, and I silently vowed, 'I am a Czech, I shall always be a Czech.'

As city after city fell to the Allies, we began to receive unbelievable reports and photographs from Nazi concentration camps. 'I forced myself to look', I wrote, 'for it would be wrong not to know and not to see these horrors. I saw open mass graves with thousands of dead bodies, I read of torture, of horrific inhuman treatment. God could not allow such monsters to conquer Europe.'

I held on to the belief that my parents had remained interned in Terezin where conditions were bad but not as desperate. I could and would not admit to myself that my own mother or father could have been the victims of such atrocities.

Eva and I were now writing to each other almost every day, sharing our anxiety, our hopes and encouraging one another. The Rainfords too were supportive and concerned. 'We shall be content with life', they wrote, 'if we live to see the end of this war and to hear that your parents are safe and well.'

On Sunday 6 May 1945 I wrote to my parents in my diary:

My dearest ones,

I want to tell you about yesterday. I woke in a fantastic

mood. Outside it was pouring, but I didn't care. At
lunchtime Eva's letter came. It made me so happy I
almost cried. The way she wrote once again reminded me
so much of you both; she has tried so hard all these years
to be your substitute. I had told her that I got a distinction
in my exams, and Eva wrote at the end, 'Thank you,
Vera, for the happiness you are giving them and me.'
Then she added, just by the way, that she had come top in
her nursing exams!

That evening there was a dance which began at seven. I
thought I would dance a little, sit out a little, but instead I
danced every single dance. It was after eight when
professor Zajicek came in to announce that the partisans
had reached Prague. Everyone clapped and shouted and
jumped for joy that Prague had been freed. I danced a
celebration polka with Harry and when it was over I was
so dizzy I couldn't see straight. Then there was a special
waltz just for those from Prague. Harry asked me to dance
again because he is from Prague and I, as he said, am as
good as 'from the suburbs'. Soon after that we listened to
the news from Czechoslovakia and my happy mood
turned to sadness. We heard that only parts of Prague had
been freed, that fighting still continues in the city, that the
partisans at the radio station are calling for help, that
German tanks are on the outskirts of Prague.

Dr Fried stopped the dance. A few people grumbled,
saying that being miserable won't help anybody.
Personally I was glad; I didn't feel like dancing any more.
I thought of my fellow countrymen, of Prague
surrounded, while the nearest help – the Americans – are
still 15 miles from Pilzen and 60 miles from Prague. I put
on my raincoat and though it was late I went out into the
rain. Somehow it helped. When I came in again, professor
Zajicek said to me 'I wanted to tell the children not to
forget to pray tonight.'

'I think, in fact I know that anyone who has ever prayed
in his life will not forget to pray tonight,' I replied.

I prayed, oh how I prayed for Prague to be freed, for it
not to be levelled to the ground, for Czech blood not to be

spilled. I prayed for you, begging God to keep you safe and to grant us our dearest wish. Please take good care of yourselves, please! If only I were to see you again, soon!

A day later the Germans signed an unconditional surrender. My diary, as usual, mirrored my feelings:

Tuesday 8 May 1945

The war is over. I can hardly believe it. We've waited so long for this day. But to me victory is not yet complete. I cannot rejoice till I hear that Prague has been liberated and that mother and father are safe.

Yesterday when we were in the middle of prep, professor Kominek came in to tell us that all hostilities had ceased and that the official announcement would be made the next day, adding that to celebrate the occasion there would be no lessons today. We danced round the study, then practically the whole of our class cycled to the Doelcoed hotel to drink to this wonderful event. But that same night the radio repeated 'Fighting continues in Prague; there are many casualties'. And our happy mood was gone.

But there was some good news. I heard that Terezin had already been liberated on the 13th of April. How I hope that mother and father were still there and that they are now free. Please God, let them survive . . .

The days passed and the month of May was almost over, but not a single child at the school had news of their loved ones at home. We were all desperate to hear and the waiting was almost unbearable. Each morning we rose with hope, each night we went to bed disappointed. In a strange way, though we shared our fears and our dreams, each one of us felt totally isolated; it seemed as if life itself hung suspended in time.

With Eva it was different. We had shared our past; she was a part of me and of my dreams. When she wrote to say that she would come and stay for a week's holiday, I was delighted. We both knew that being together would make the waiting easier.

28 May 1945

Eva is gone. I can hardly believe it. The week simply
flew by. I think this was the nicest time I've ever spent
with her – we felt so very close. We understood each other
so well, agreed about almost everything, and we didn't
quarrel – not even once. She's only just left and I miss her
already.

We had a lovely week. I found her a room on a farm
where the people are really friendly. The teachers turned
up trumps and let me off lessons whenever possible – I
think they all realised how much Eva and I need each
other just now. At school everyone likes her and says how
attractive she is.

I liked it best when we were on our own, walking in the
hills, sitting by the river, talking and talking, remembering . . .
One evening we reread all our letters from home. Our
parents wrote so beautifully. Will they see many changes
in me? Will they know me, will they love me as I am now?
Surely they will! The only thing that matters is to be
together.

This morning I got up at six so I could spend one more
hour with Eva before we said goodbye. I hated to see her
go.

Thursday 31 May 1945

I have neglected you, diary. So many times during these
past few days I've looked at your empty pages, but I felt
despondent and listless and found it hard to concentrate.
The same applied to reading and school work – my
intentions were good but I always ended up gazing out of
the window, thinking of mother and father. I couldn't
settle down to anything. Each night I fell asleep with their
names on my lips, each morning I rose with the same
question on my mind: will there be some news today?

This morning a letter came from Eva. Somehow I knew
it contained special news. I scanned the first few lines and
there it was:

'And now the most important news. I have had a letter
from Auntie Berta's friend, Mr Herczka, who lives in

London. He's had a message from Stockholm which says that mother and father are alive and well, and we are not to worry. That's all. I am terribly thrilled, but this is not enough. I want to see that letter for myself, and I want to know more. I shall go up to London tomorrow and will write to you the moment I return.'

To say I was delighted would be an understatement. I cried with joy and thanked dear God for hearing my prayers. This is the most important, the most wonderful day of my life. Yet I am almost afraid to believe it is true. When I hold a letter in their own handwriting there will be no more doubts in my mind and my happiness will be complete.

Everyone here is so thrilled for me. I am the first child in the school to hear. Even the teachers are coming up to me to hug and congratulate me. Many of them are also waiting for news. As it happens, today the village was celebrating V.E. Day; the celebration had to be postponed because of a whooping cough epidemic. We were all invited, and the postponement suited me fine, because now I really had something to celebrate. There was food and music and dancing, and I was in seventh heaven. I feel truly blessed, my beloved *maminko, tatinku,* and I thank God a thousand times for granting us our dearest wish.

Friday 1 June 1945

I am turning to you, dear diary, for my heart is heavy and aching, and my thoughts are all jumbled and confused; they are going round and round in my head like snow flakes in a storm.

I was so happy yesterday when I heard mother and father are alive. It gave me such joy just to whisper their names, I talked to them, smiled at them.

This evening the school received the list of survivors from Belsen. I was horrified to find mother's and Auntie Berta's names on that list. It must be them, because although mother is listed under 'D' and auntie under 'K' they have been given consecutive numbers: Diamant Irma

CABLEGRAM VIA NORTHERN

THE GREAT NORTHERN TELEGRAPH CO.
(LIMITED) OF DENMARK.

Lith. C. 1027. 1929—5,000,000. Löh.

Direct, speedy and reliable connection with CHINA, HONGKONG, JAPAN, MACAO, MANILA, U.S.S.R., FINLAND, LATVIA, ESTONIA, LITHUANIA, POLAND, SWEDEN, DENMARK, FAROE ISLANDS, ICELAND, and GREENLAND.

N. 54
N

RECD. 2/5 MAY 19 42

BY: GW

HBG

STOCKHOLM GS1634 12 25 1610

HERCZKA BELSEZEPARK 58 LONDON-NW3

IRMA BERTA ARE WELL CONGRATULATION LETTER SEND = HERZFELD +

(household) no. 01818813, and Kestner Berta (clerk) no.
01818812. I was stunned to learn that they've had to
endure the brutalities of that concentration camp, yet
relieved to know that they have survived. But the name of
father, our dear beloved father was not there. I hope, I so
hope that he is on another list, that he too is alive. After
yesterday's happiness all this is such a blow. I thought they
had both survived, and Auntie Berta too, that they had
been kept in Terezin – and now I know they were in
Belsen which I've been told was one of the worst camps –
and I don't even know if father was there too and if he is
still alive . . .

I am numb with shock. I can't take it in. Only yesterday
such joyful news . . . I hope against hope it will still turn
out to be true. I flung myself onto my bunk and I cried and
cried and this time my tears were not tears of joy. I love
them both. I so longed to see the four of us together.
Maybe I will, who knows . . .

Yet I must be strong, I must have courage and faith in
myself that if the very worst were to happen I could look
my grief straight in the eye. But *tato, tatinku*, I want you
so . . .

Sunday 3 June 1945

Eva has just phoned. The message Mr Herczka had
received had been sent by mother and auntie on the 25th
of March. The man in Stockholm added: 'Mazeltov!'
Surely he wouldn't congratulate us if he knew father had
not survived?

Thursday 7 June 1945

I can write only briefly for I am trying very hard to
knuckle down to my studies. The end of the year exams
will be upon us in two to three weeks, and I so want to
bring mother (and hopefully father) a good report. But it
is so difficult to concentrate.

Today I received a letter from Bloomsbury House.
They had a card from one Irma Diamant who was
enquiring about Vera Diamant. 'Is she a relative?' they

asked. 'She is my mother,' I wrote back straightaway, asking for the card and also if they have any news of father. I enclosed a short note to mother too, in case they could forward it. I know that any news from us, no matter how brief, would be the most wonderful tonic.

Eva is confident father is alive but I would rather be prepared for the worst, and then be joyfully surprised. It seems so strange that no one mentions him, that there is not one word about him or from him. I do so hope that Eva is right, that my worry is unfounded. Whatever happens, mother has survived, and in that knowledge lies my joy and happiness. Now that I know she has had to endure Belsen, my longing to be with her, to love and care for her, is stronger than ever. No matter what awaits me – hard work, heartache, poverty maybe – I can face anything, I am ready to tackle anything, for mother will be there. And though I can't help feeling unsettled and a little apprehensive, I am not unhappy. I am so fortunate, so rich! I have been given back my mother – and there are so many children here who will probably never see their mothers again.

Saturday 16 June 1945

Dearest *maminko*,

It is such a beautiful day! The sun is shining brightly and I am sitting alone in a flower-strewn meadow, in my hand the note you and auntie sent to Stockholm, and the card which came through the Red Cross. I kiss each word, each precious letter written in your very own hand – and I so long to kiss and hug you!

But someone must have made a mistake, because father's name is not mentioned. I feel so uneasy about him. I keep telling myself that perhaps he was interned somewhere else and that we shall hear from him soon. That would make me the happiest person in the whole world. I don't know why, but I keep remembering some words father once wrote to me – and such unimportant words too: 'I am trying to take a nap, but some cheeky fly keeps buzzing round and round my head'. I can see it so

Richard Herzfeld

Stockholm
Sveavey 28 – 30
Schweden.

Please write the children
that we are healthy there, we
have forgotten her adress. Many
kisses

Irma and Berta
Diamant,

clearly, father, spread out on the verandah couch, and
that impertinent fly. And for some reason, whenever I
think of it, I burst into tears.

I'd like to dream tonight that the four of us are strolling
along the banks of the Elbe; Eva and father deep in conversation, you smiling, and holding my hand. It is such a beautiful
vision I hardly dare believe it could ever come true . . .

                                          21 June 1945
Dearest *maminko*,
I am right in the middle of examinations and I have no
time to spare but I simply had to write to you. One girl,
Dasa, had news today that the Germans have murdered
her mother. She is so unhappy! Poor Dasa! I feel for her
so deeply, and I thank God and fate for not dealing me a
similar blow. Luckily Dasa has a kind aunt and uncle who
took care of her here in Britain; she will now return with
them to Czechoslovakia. But what a dreadful bitter
disappointment.

                                   Tuesday 3 July 1945
This is my last day of being sixteen. In a matter of hours
I'll be a year older. How time flies! It is six years to the day
since I met the Rainfords for the first time. I am so much
older, wiser and more experienced now. I can hardly
believe that in a few short weeks I shall be on my way
home . . .

I shall hate saying goodbye to this loving family, to my
school and to England – to everything that has formed the
pattern of my life these past few years. I shall miss it all,
particularly the school, but then the reason for its
existence was to prepare us for our return home. Some of
the children whose parents or other relatives are here are
not going back – at least not just yet. But I and others like
me who have no family in Britain are being repatriated by
the school. I'm not quite sure when my turn will come.
The school will send for me when it is time.

I am now back at the Rainfords looking out at houses
instead of the rolling Welsh hills, hearing Mummy

Rainford's voice instead of the shouts and laughter of the children. We had such a lovely end of term! It was extra special, for we knew that there was no next term, and that from then on we would all go our separate ways. That part of it was rather sad, of course, for we've been one big happy family for so long it seems hardly possible that some of us may never see each other again.

I wonder if I'll ever return to Llanwrtyd Wells, once I leave Britain? We gave a concert for our Welsh friends before we broke up, and it turned out a very sentimental evening. We also held our last dance, and this time all the teachers joined in – I even danced with professor Krusina and Havlicek, the headmaster. Everyone was so nice and friendly and no one wanted the evening to end. Then there was the school's very last play, one of Capek's, and once again I played opposite Bobby. Goodness knows how I ever managed to learn my part! Talking of learning, I did pass with distinction, and so did five others in my class – in fact the results of my form were the best in the school.

For a while I almost stopped worrying about father, there was so much going on, so much to do, and the days flew by so fast. Those last weeks were almost like a dream, but I shall remember them always.

Something unexpected happened at the end of term. Just when I had succeeded in putting Walter out of my mind and heart, I had a letter from him, right out of the blue. He said that he hadn't forgotten me, that he had read my letters over and over again, that he now realised that he'd made a terrible mistake not to have kept in contact. He gave no explanation for his silence – perhaps he has none. But he was so anxious to hear from me that he actually sent eight stamps for my reply! And of course I did reply because I wanted to see him, though I've no intention of falling for him again. But after all, this is my last holiday in England, we get on well and we can have a lot of fun together. I'm so glad he is still in Liverpool.

We've met several times already, but I tell you, diary: my heart won't break when we have to part. I like him a

Abernant Hotel, the school's Welsh haven, as it was
in 1943, and the village which opened its heart to us

Auntie Berta, Mila and her little daughter, Vera

Prague 1946:

A holiday snap of the same trio, with me added  The same year, mountaineering in the Tatras

lot, but I'm not as keen as I was, and I'm more critical too.
I suspect that his feelings towards me are stronger and
deeper than they were at school. I am sorry about that as
it may upset him when I leave. For me the situation is
quite different: I am going to mother, and my love and
heart belong to her.

Last Sunday the weather was fabulous, so Walter and I
cycled to Freshfield. The sea was a beautiful clear blue
and it sparkled in the sun, edged with soft white sand and
bright greenery. We were lucky, the tide was in. We
ran straight into the sea, and it was the nicest swim I've
ever had. Wave after wave, as high as a house, swung us
up and down, up and down, like a giant see-saw. Now and
then the waves tossed me up in the air, and then foamed
and crashed beneath me as if they were laughing at me.
And I laughed and shouted with the waves, drank the
salty water and dived through them like a fish. By the time
we ran back to the beach we were quite exhausted, so we
threw ourselves onto the hot sand.

The lovely hours we spent together that day proved to
me again what a sincere boy Walter is. Neither of us is
calling what we feel for each other love. Perhaps in a year
or two it could turn into love if he eventually returns to
Czechoslovakia. Who knows? For the moment what we
have is a strong firm friendship. This is all I want and all I
am prepared to give. At present there is no room for
anyone but my parents in my heart.

Thursday 12 July 1945

Dearest *maminko,*
I haven't written to you lately in my diary but I have
sent you a long letter with Dasa who is already on her way
to Prague. I long for further news of you, and of father,
though the very thought of what may have happened to
him fills me with fear. Thank God you have come
through, that He is returning us to you! Only a few brief
weeks and I shall be with you at last.

For the moment I am basking in the affection of the
Rainfords and all my friends. Everyone is being terribly

generous and kind. The Rainfords would part with their
last penny to make sure I have all I need for my return,
and Auntie Margery is determined to send me back with
almost as good a wardrobe as you provided me with when
I came all those years ago. I am staying with her at the
moment, and she is working furiously at her sewing
machine. In her enthusiasm she has almost cleaned out
Moyra's wardrobe; I've even been given the coat Moyra
wore as an ambulance driver so that I should have a good
warm coat for the Czech winter. Auntie Margery is so
good to me; I just wish she didn't preach all the time. She
is after saving everyone's soul. I am religious in my own
way. I believe it is my duty to help my fellow man and I
have faith in God. But I feel closest to Him when I am
alone with my own thoughts. I know He exists because He
has watched over you; though you have suffered so, He
has spared you, and I thank Him each night for hearing
my constant prayer.

                                        Wednesday 18 July 1945
I have no words to express what I feel . . . Thoughts whirl
in my head, I feel as though I am choking, my eyes are
burning, my brain refuses to understand. Though it is past
midnight I know I shan't rest or sleep until I have found
some comfort in you, diary.

    This evening I came home late from visiting a friend; I
felt happy, almost carefree. The moment I got in I asked
as usual if there was any post. There was one letter – from
Eva. I was seized with a strange and terrifying
premonition. I ripped the envelope open. The first thing
that struck me was the neatness of her handwriting, as if
she were taking exceptional care. Right from the
beginning I realised that Eva was slowly and gently
leading up to something very important.

    But it hurts, oh how it hurts . . . *Maminka,* our dearest
maminka for whose life I have thanked God every day,
maminka, whom I wanted to surround with laughter and love,
whom I wanted to work and care for – she is no more. She
died of typhus in Belsen two days after the end of the war.

Where were you, God?

My dearest sister broke the news to me so gently, so carefully. 'Outside the sun is shining', she wrote, 'smiling at a world that has seen so much sorrow and suffering. Perhaps this is God's way of showing us that beauty and peace exist up above, that He is looking down on us, saying "Believe in me and you shall come to me one day. Here you shall all be together; here you shall forget the pain of the world."

'Are you brave, little sister? Have you faith and strength? Of course you have! You are mother's and father's child, and mine too, in a way. How I wish I could spare you from hearing what I must tell you now, but I cannot. *Verusko,* mother lived to see the liberation of Belsen by the British army, she lived to see the end of the war and she rejoiced in our victory. She was not in Nazi hands but in kind British hands, in their hospital, when she died of typhus. *Verusko,* look up bravely at the sky and whisper "Thank you, God, for letting her see the end of the war".

Actress renowned, don't fail in your role now! The audience applauds, you have to play on until the curtain goes down. Most of the acts you have yet to play, for the rest of your life lies before you, and all through it mother will be so close, so very close. Can you hear her whispering to God, "Do not forsake them, give them strength and courage, make them have faith that one day we shall meet up here, and then we shall be together forever."'

Eva wrote more, much more. Oh God, help us!

Auntie Margery and her family are full of sympathy and they keep assuring me that I will always have a home with them. But theirs is not the home I want! I cannot bear their sympathy nor their tears. I need to be alone with my grief.

Apart from the devastating knowledge that I shan't ever see my dearest mother one thought stands clear in my

mind: I must not waver, I must stick to my decision to go
back home. It will be hard, so very hard now, but I am
young, I want to help to rebuild my country, I want to
prove that I can be independent, unafraid of hard work
and an uncertain future. The world seems so lonely, so
empty at this moment. But though I am alone, though
I may be an orphan, I still have Eva. *Maminko,* if Heaven
exists, you surely are there, far removed from the miseries
of this world. Your face smiles at me from your picture
and I am trying to smile back. I shall always send my
kisses through the sun and the stars, and I shall do my
utmost to earn the right to follow you up there one day.
Perhaps you have found father . . . I feel so desolate, and
desperately unhappy, but I know I must not grieve
because that would cause you unhappiness too. Life
will go on and I have to take whatever comes, and I will
not go under, that I promise you. As your and father's
daughter I shall go through life with my head held high, I
shall always feel your presence and will try never to let
you down.

I think I shed the last remnants of my girlhood that night
of 18 July. And then barely a week later we were dealt the
final blow which confirmed our worst fears. A telegram
came from Auntie Berta to say that neither mother nor
father had survived. She alone had returned to Prague . . .
   'Why had fate treated us so cruelly?' I kept asking myself,
first pretending that it was going to give us back both our
parents, making us believe in our life together, in our joint
future, and then destroying our happiness so brutally, bit by
bit, until all our hopes crumbled and crashed around us and
there was nothing left but emptiness?
   Eva and I tried to comfort one another; I was touched by
everyone's sincere efforts to cheer and help me. I tried to
draw strength from the words of the Methodist minister:
'Still lives, still here, still yours, still His.' But I felt numb,
devoid of all feeling, unable to laugh or cry. With deep
sadness in my heart I looked towards the empty future, the
last remnants of my dreams shattered.

Auntie Berta sent another telegram advising Eva and me to remain in England.

I ignored it. How could I stay? I had never really considered that eventuality. At this crucial point in my life I could not envisage a future anywhere but in Czechoslovakia. My patriotism, nurtured by the school, burned fiercely. My country needed me, my country would welcome me. No matter how painful life without my parents might be, I owed it to their memory, I owed it to my country – it was my duty to return.

Eva's final nursing exams were not for several months yet, and though she did not try to dissuade me, she suggested I delay my departure until then, knowing that if we returned together, the homecoming would be easier for us both. But I was too impatient to wait. I wanted to be in Prague for the beginning of the new school year; I was anxious to find out if any other members of our family had survived, and I was desperate to learn all I could about the fate of my parents. I consoled myself with the thought that at least I had Auntie Berta, mother's own sister, wating for me. I would not be quite alone.

She had told us that she thought father had been shot on a death march, but no one could say exactly where or when. I hardly dared to hold on to this glimmer of hope. But what if he wasn't dead after all? What if father was in some hospital, too ill to contact us? I had to go home!

At the beginning of August I was told to report back at the school immediately, as my group was scheduled to be repatriated in two or three weeks' time. One or two small groups of children and staff had already left; others were to follow later. In the frenzy of last-minute activities such as shopping for items which I knew were scarce in Prague, packing and saying goodbye, I hardly had time to feel sorry for myself, or sentimental about Walter. I didn't tell him about my parents until he came to say goodbye. The grim news had a strange effect on him; although he was terribly upset on my behalf, he seemed withdrawn, almost distant and very hesitant about his own future.

I couldn't understand the change in him, but then I was

still completely unaware of his German origins. I wouldn't have held this against him, because his parents were Social Democrats who were also persecuted by the Nazis. I learned the truth after my return to Prague from Walter's friend who had received only one letter from him with no return address. He told me that the death of my parents made Walter feel guiltier than ever for being a German, and he could not face me again. Instead of returning to Czechoslovakia as he had planned he chose to go to Germany to work in the displaced persons' camps. I never saw or heard of him again.

Saying goodbye to the Rainfords was very, very hard. By then they were very much my family, and as I embraced each of them I wondered fleetingly whether I had made the right decision, I was leaving so much love behind. I drew comfort from the knowledge that their door would always remain open and that I would always be welcomed back if I failed to find happiness in my own country.

Olga wrote to say goodbye. I learned from her that her parents had also perished, in Auschwitz. Unlike me, she was not going to Prague but America where she had an aunt who had promised to look after her if anything were to happen to her parents. I was sad for her, and sorry to hear we would be so far apart, yet glad that Olga had someone to go to – someone who cared.

Back at the school I found out that every one of the ten children in my group, which included my friends Jula, Alice and Margit, had suffered the same loss. As far as we knew, not a single parent had survived; we were all orphans. Alice, Margit and I were more fortunate than most, for all three of us had escaped to Britain with our older sisters. Many of the others had had their whole families wiped out.

Except for a couple of teachers our small group was alone in the school which was no longer a school. The large building, which for years had rung to the laughter of children was now strangely silent, soon to be converted back into the modern elegant Abernant Lake Hotel.

Happily for us, Miss Mac was there, full of concern and sympathy, giving practical help wherever it was needed.

Alice's sister had left England as soon as the war ended and had made her way to Terezin where she helped to clear the ghetto. She had married in Britain, and now she sent Alice a telegram which read, 'Expecting a baby, please bring baby clothes', for such items at that time were unobtainable in Czechoslovakia. It was Miss Mac, of course, who gave Alice the money to buy them. When Jula had trouble fitting his worldly possessions into his small battered case, she gave him hers, and I was given beautiful soft wool of a quality unknown during the war years to knit my aunt a warm cardigan. But the greatest gift was her cheerful compassionate presence, her warm friendship and moral support.

The ten of us felt somewhat lost in the large empty school and we spent most of our time out of doors, and in the village. Our local friend, Jim Jones, intent on cheering us up, piled the whole crowd into his minibus on the last day and took us for a picnic. That same night, back at the school, we lit a bonfire in the woods. Cloaked by darkness, but with the moon and the stars bright in the sky, we sat round the fire with Jim and other local friends. As we munched the snack we had prepared and downed the cider Jim had supplied, we reminisced and sang Welsh songs, Czech songs, English songs, and waxed more and more sentimental.

We were still there at the first sign of dawn, anxious not to bring to an end the last precious hours in this peaceful little corner of Wales which had given us such a happy home. Little did we know then of what lay ahead, the struggles we would be faced with, the joys and disappointments which for many of us would follow.

As the stars and the moon slowly faded and I sat staring into the dying flames, the memory of a similar scene flashed across my mind when, so long ago, I had sat by another bonfire in a holiday camp by the river Sazava. The tears poured down my cheeks as I remembered the very homesick nine-year-old who so proudly said to her mother when she came to fetch her: 'I didn't cry. I am a diamond. I only shed pearls . . .'

PART II

Where Is My Home?

8

The Sad Homecoming

27 AUGUST 1945 announced itself, as if in celebration, with a clear blue sky and a dazzling sun, for this was the day my group was being finally repatriated. We were being flown home courtesy of the RAF in their wartime bomber which, for several weeks now, had been making trips from Britain to Prague with cargos of Czech refugees.

Neither I nor any of the other nine children squatting with me on the floor of the plane's fuselage had ever flown before and this, coupled with the knowledge that at long last we were homeward-bound made our first flight a truly memorable one.

The crew, infected by our excitement, were talkative and friendly, and eventually allowed each of us in turn to sit in the gun turret and look at the view. My turn came when we were over Cologne. As I saw a thin cathedral spire pointing up accusingly from the ruins, the sole reminder of what that city used to be, I wondered fleetingly whether the crew of our Halifax bomber had flown this route before, laden with bombs, on a mission to kill and destroy . . .

And then at last we were crossing over Prague, some of us crammed in the cockpit. Almost untouched by bombs, it looked beautiful slumbering in the noon haze, with not one, but hundreds of spires reaching into the sky. The river Vltava, spanned by numerous bridges – all intact, not destroyed like those across the Rhine – wound its way through the heart of the city, then zigzagged like a shimmering snake through the hills and out of sight. And Hradcany Castle, as magnificent as ever, towered above it all. My heart swelled with pride and emotion. This was the capital of my country. I had, at long last, come home . . .

I had dreamed of this moment so many times, but in my dreams mother and father had been waiting for me. The time had come to bury my dreams and face reality, yet I still could not envisage a future or a home without them . . . Clutching the same rucksack which had accompanied me to

England in 1939 and which, apart from a few personal items, was packed with soap, toothpaste and cigarettes which we had been told were the best currency, I tumbled out of the plane into a completely different world from the one I had left behind.

There was no one to meet me, but then there was no one waiting for any of us with the exception of Alice, whose sister had arrived in Prague earlier; aware that in those early post-war days communication between Czechoslovakia and England was almost non-existent, she trudged to the airport day after day just in case Alice appeared.

'Please try and contact my aunt and tell her I am here,' I said, suddenly apprehensive of what Auntie Berta would say when she found out I had ignored her advice to remain in Britain.

I hardly had time to give Alice's sister the slip of paper on which I had scribbled auntie's address, as I was hustled into an improvised open bus heading for a repatriation centre. The centre was a school, converted into dormitories with long rows of bunk beds. It served as a quarantine station and a temporary home for those who had nowhere else to go. We looked and felt somewhat out of place, for we were well dressed, well nourished and healthy, in sharp contrast to the other occupants, survivors from concentration and labour camps. I could hardly bear to look at those pitiful figures whose very presence was such a painful reminder of my parents' suffering, and I was impatient to get away from there.

Although, as war orphans, we were now the responsibility of the state, no one seemed particularly interested in us. When I questioned the man who appeared to be in charge, and explained that I had a relative to go to, he merely snapped that we all had to be medically vetted and would have to remain in quarantine until then, like those who had come from the camps. Protesting loudly, we produced certificates to prove that before leaving Britain we had been immunised against all conceivable diseases, and also confirm that we were in the best of health. The man barely glanced at them, shrugged and said: 'Rules are rules, and here you will stay.' So we stayed, but we didn't like it one bit.

I was lucky. Auntie Berta received the message and came to fetch me the very next day. Happily, no one objected, which confirmed that the main reason we were being kept at the centre was that the authorities were at a loss what to do with us. As I learned later, my schoolmates who returned to find that none of their relatives had survived were eventually placed in orphanages or with families. Those over seventeen were declared officially of age, provided with hostel accommodation, then left, more or less, to fend for themselves. I really was lucky in more ways than one to have Auntie Berta!

I shall never forget that first meeting. I had said goodbye as a child, but now I faced her as a young woman. No child could ever have felt the compassion and love she awakened in me as she appeared in the doorway, looking so frail that a breath of wind could waft her away. But it was not her painfully thin body, nor her drawn white face which shocked me. It was her eyes which, in spite of her evident pleasure at the sight of me, were deep pools of unspeakable sadness.

'Verusko, Verusko, is it really you?' she cried, as I ran towards her. And as I put my arms around her I vowed that I would do my utmost to erase that haunted look from her eyes.

That was the only time I ever saw her cry; the only time she put her arms around me and held me close. Remembering how undemonstrative she had always been, I treasured that moment and knew instinctively from that one embrace how glad she was to see me and that there would be no reproaches that I had ignored her advice and returned.

To my surprise, auntie did not take me to the spacious flat she had shared all her life with my grandparents. A butcher who had a shop in the same block had moved in there with his family, and now flatly refused to move out. Far from being glad that she, once a regular customer, had survived the concentration camp, he resented the fact she had returned and claimed what was rightfully hers. He didn't care that the furniture and almost everything in the flat belonged to my aunt; such details were of no consequence.

The Prague housing office showed the same cool disinterest. The housing situation was pretty desperate and there were thousands of homeless people. The authorities were not prepared to evict a family of four from a flat and hand it over to two single females, whatever the circumstances. They were not concerned with the rights and wrongs of the situation, nor with the moral issues. 'Your case will come under review; in the meantime, find yourself somewhere to stay, or we'll give you a bed in a hostel' was the usual response.

I therefore found myself in what was to be my home for the next few months – a two-roomed flat which belonged to mother and auntie's younger cousin Karel and his wife Mila, who had miraculously survived the holocaust. Although we had no room of our own, and my aunt and I even had to share a bed, I felt very much at home there. I was with relatives, real relatives who had known my whole family. I loved to hear tales of mother's and father's youth, especially of their courtship which had blossomed during holidays spent at Karel's country home in the Krkonose mountains. Even at the age of ten Karel had been quick to appreciate mother's beauty and gentleness, and father's roguish charm; he was often their unseen but devoted companion.

I warmed to Mila and Karel all the more because they, like my aunt, had at one stage been interned with my parents. As yet they could not bring themselves to tell me of those terrible years; their experiences were too recent, too painful. And, looking back, I don't think I could have absorbed or coped with the full truth just then. I was given a few plain hard facts: prior to being deported, Auntie Berta had been arrested by the Gestapo and imprisoned in Prague. The shock killed grandmother but at least she was spared the horror of a concentration camp. Grandfather died in Terezin, sick and alone. Tommy and Honza, my two cousins who almost made it to England in 1939, managed to survive the war, but, like mother, they too died of typhus in Belsen. Auntie Berta nursed and lost all three: Tommy on 1 May – his sixteenth birthday – mother on 10 May, Honza on 21 May. Each one died in her arms. Is it any wonder that grief and depression were her constant companions for the rest of her days? Tommy and Honza's parents died in Auschwitz, as did father's two sisters and their families. Our only other surviving relative was cousin Heda, who had escaped during a transfer from one camp to another and was hidden by some kind people until the war ended. As for father – there was still no proof of his death. 'Missing, presumed dead' was the unconfirmed verdict.

I tried not to dwell on the tragedies of the past but to concentrate on coping with and settling into my new life. I knew that this would not be easy and that there were many hurdles to cross. Getting accustomed to a new school was the first – one I had to face within days of my return, at the start of the autumn term. I still had two years of study before I could take my matriculation, and I was confident that the education I had received in Britain would be more than adequate to enable me to hold my own in the gymnasium (grammar school) that I joined.

All the same, as I entered my new form for the first time, I was more than a little nervous, and all the more when I saw my fellow-pupils eyeing me with undisguised less than friendly curiosity. I was therefore greatly relieved to see two familiar faces among the thirty or so strange ones. Honza and Seppi, my old classmates from Abernant, were there too, looking every bit as nervous and uncomfortable as I was feeling.

I suppose it was understandable that the other pupils looked askance at us. Hitler had swept all Jews out of their lives years ago, and as far as they knew, they were never coming back. Seeing three Jewish children in their class must have been quite a shocking surprise.

To our disappointment and dismay, the teachers treated us no better. Some were friendly and kind, but others uninterested and aloof as if they resented our presence and the fact that we had spent the war years in comparative comfort and safety while they had had to suffer the hardships of Nazi occupation. Those years, during which they had to toe the German line in order to keep their jobs, had left their mark. Conditioned by anti-semitic propaganda, they were not particularly inclined now to go out of their way to make any returning Jewish children feel welcome or at home, even though they knew we had lost our homes and were orphans.

After the friendly informality of our school in Wales, we were hurt and puzzled by this almost hostile attitude, and we worked hard to gain the confidence and favour of both masters and fellow-students, desperately wanting to be accepted; but although the situation gradually improved, we never quite made it. This was the first time in post-war Czechoslovakia that I felt the stigma of being Jewish.

There were other problems that had to be solved. The top priority was to find somewhere else for Auntie Berta and myself to live. Karel and Mila, determined to put the past behind them and to start afresh, were already expecting a child, and I knew that once the baby was born there would not be enough room for us all. Our only hope was auntie's old flat, but even here we continued to draw a blank.

Seeing my aunt's distress and despondency every time she returned from the housing office, I decided to apply my youthful vigour to the problem and to tackle the authorities myself. I bombarded them with telephone calls, letters and visits, stressing the urgency of the situation, still believing naïvely in British 'fair play'.

One day at last we were rewarded with a reply. The case had been reviewed and yes, it was decided that Miss Kestner had a right to her old flat. But as she was the only one of the original occupants still alive, she was entitled to a single room only and the smallest one at that. The authorities refused to take into account that Eva would be joining us shortly, but as Miss Kestner was now the legal guardian of one Vera Diamant, her orphaned niece, who would be living with her, they were prepared to throw in the tiny kitchen, and to allow us the use of the toilet, but not the bathroom; that would remain exclusively for the use of the butcher's family.

I could hardly believe the irony and injustice of it all; but we desperately needed a roof over our heads and had to accept that small concession. And so, one grey wintry day we moved to the cold little room which could never be warmed and brightened by the sun, for it faced north and opened on to a dark courtyard. I looked around the shabby room, filled with the butcher's cast-offs. He had the audacity to keep grandfather's choicest pieces of furniture, even his favourite chair.

'Don't get yourself upset,' I pleaded, seeing my aunt's sorrowful face, trying hard to sound bright and cheerful. 'We'll make it into a nice home, you'll see.' But inside I was seething with anger and indignation. How could someone who had suffered such hardships be treated so shamefully by her own people?

There was yet another important hurdle to cross: I had to find the courage and strength to go back to Celakovice, my home town, the scene of my happy childhood. Week by week, I postponed the trip. Even my life in Prague, where we had never lived, seemed so unbearably empty without my parents. How could I face the place where every street, every face would be a vivid reminder of my lost happiness?

Yet I longed to go, to see Marta and our family friends, to walk back in time, to suffer the bitter-sweet pain of remembering. There was another, more practical reason too: prior to being deported, mother had distributed some savings and valuables and a few personal effects among several friends for safe-keeping. She had given auntie all the details before she died, and auntie was now anxious that I should claim and collect what was rightfully Eva's and mine.

'Please let me go on my own,' I said, not wanting her to see the tears I knew would come, and to inflict upon her the burden of my emotions. Besides, this was one hurdle I had to cross on my own, without anyone's help. And so one Saturday I finally took the train and sat on the same uncomfortable seats on which I had fidgeted Sunday after Sunday on the way to and from my grandparents' flat. As the train chugged along the familiar route, I thought of the child I had been then, and felt much older than my seventeen years. My happy time in Britain seemed a lifetime away, with me a different person in a different world. My return to Czechoslovakia was proving more difficult than my arrival in

England had been. There I had been accepted, here I felt almost an outsider. Yet this was my country, this was where I belonged . . .

The station was as I remembered it, and so was the station master. I sneaked past him, and walked unrecognised along the same uneven pavement of the main street, past the cinema-cum-gym-cum-dance-hall I had so often visited, past the shops where I used to shop for mother, and right under the very window of Marta's one-roomed flat. Oblivious to everyone and everything around me, I did not raise my head even as I passed the wide, arched entrance to our house.

I crossed the road into the town square, deserted on this cold morning, and sat on the wooden seat, staring fixedly at the unkempt borders choked with weeds where a few late autumn flowers bravely fought for survival. The quaint old town hall and my old school were behind me, hidden by the leafy branches of giant chestnut trees.

Then, slowly, I forced my eyes upwards to look at the house opposite. Oh, how battered and sad it looked, how uncared for, with dirty windows, peeling paint and gaping holes in the wall where the balcony had been. Was it only six years ago when that same house had been so white, with colourful flower-filled window boxes? Our house, my home, which held so much happiness and love.

As if in a trance I walked over to the entrance, climbed the familiar staircase and rang the bell on what was once my own front door. A strange woman answered. 'I am Vera Diamant,' I whispered. 'I used to live here.' She nodded, and gestured me to come in.

The verandah was the first room on the left – a sunny room in which I used to play and where father always took his Saturday afternoon naps. Bits of bicycle now littered the uncarpeted floor. A man and a boy looked up at me questioningly. I slipped past them and opened the door leading to the toilet. And there on the wall, clearly visible, were the words I had written in my childish hand: 'Goodbye, my lavatory'. And I remembered father refusing to have the toilet decorated until after my safe return. 'I am here,' my heart cried, 'but where are you, dearest father?'

I turned and fled, running through the streets to the banks
of the river Elbe where I buried my face in the dying grass
and cried the bitter tears that had to be shed, the tears I did
not want Auntie Berta, or anyone to see.

That first hour had to be mine and my parents' alone. It
would not have withstood intruders. My heart was a shrine
to their memory, filled with my love for them. More
composed now, but feeling drained and desolate I walked
back towards the town, hoping that I was now ready to face
the people I knew.

Suddenly a young girl appeared, a chubby girl, with dark
hair flying in the breeze; when she saw me, her anxious,
pretty face broke into a wide dimpled smile.

It was unmistakably Marta, my childhood friend, my old
shadow. A passer-by had recognised me and, remembering
our close friendship, had knocked on Marta's door.

With shrieks of delight we fell into each other's arms and
burst into tears. She was like a breath of fresh air, a ray of
sunshine in a world which for those first two months had
seemed cheerless and grey.

Auntie Berta had already told me how loyal Marta had
been after I had left for England – how she visited my
parents every day, at some risk to herself, since contact
between Aryans and Jews was strictly forbidden. At one
point the local constable warned Marta's father that such
action was dangerous, but his affection and esteem for our
family and his disgust at seeing my parents shunned and
victimised made him turn a blind eye to his daughter's daily
visits.

Her company must have given mother and father great
comfort during that lonely, frightening time when many
friends, fearing for their own safety, avoided them, even
crossing to the opposite side of the street if they saw them
walking along the pavement, wearing the compulsory yellow
star.

I certainly had a lot to thank Marta for . . . Talking
excitedly, we walked arm in arm, and almost before we
realised it we were standing in front of my house. With
Marta at my side, I plucked up courage to step into the

courtyard. There was no trace of machinery, stock or furniture in the buildings which had housed our office, wine production and warehouse. They had been put to other uses and everything movable had been confiscated by the Germans after father's arrest. No one would have known that this had once been a flourishing wine and spirit business.

We looked around the courtyard which used to be our favourite playground. Even the large wooden tub which made a perfect paddling pool in summer, and the old broken-down cart we used as a see-saw were gone. I peered into the empty stable, which still smelt of Vana. I could almost hear him neighing in happy anticipation of the carrot or sugar in my pocket. I looked wistfully across to the hay loft, remembering all the strays and my own kittens for which this had been home.

As if reading my thoughts, Marta asked if I would like to see one of my kittens. I nodded, and she led me to the inn where father had spent many pleasant hours playing cards and drinking beer with the locals. A plump tabby cat was soon purring contentedly on my lap as I stroked her soft coat, while the owner of the inn stood discreetly by, waiting to welcome me home. As I hugged the lone four-legged survivor of our household and saw the genuine compassion and friendship in the innkeeper's eyes, I realised that for the first time since my arrival in Czechoslovakia I was beginning to feel at home.

It was a memorable, highly emotional, bitter-sweet day during which many doors opened to me, and behind each one I found a warm welcome. Everyone exclaimed how grown-up I was – a real English miss they called me – how like my mother now (this pleased me greatly, for she was beautiful, and I was not). They talked about the past and about my parents with such sincerity and fondness that I felt myself warming towards them.

The owner of the sweet shop where I used to spend my pocket money came running after me, in his hand a bar of my favourite chocolate. 'You see, I haven't forgotten,' he cried, beaming at me.

'I've got something for you too,' said a round-faced country woman, whom I only knew vaguely, and she proudly produced Eva's bicycle, so clean and shiny that it looked brand new. Mother had given it to her daughter who was Eva's friend. She had hardly used it, but polished it every week, in case Eva or I decided to return.

That old lady, a comparative stranger, was not on my aunt's list of special friends with whom mother and father had left their most prized possessions for safe-keeping. I knew I would have to see them and ask for what was mine, but I didn't want to risk spoiling what had turned out to be such a happy day, so I left that particular task for the following day, when Auntie Berta was to join me. I had phoned her and pleaded to be allowed to stay overnight, hating the thought of returning to Prague and our dismal little room sooner than I had to. Marta had invited me to share her bed, and her mother was already busy cooking one of my favourite dishes for supper – sweet dumplings filled with plums, swimming in curd cheese and butter . . .

I knew full well that I was looking at my town through rose-tinted glasses. I didn't want to be reminded that there was corruption, greed and anti-semitism here too, that during the occupation some had turned traitor and collaborated with the Nazis. I had been told that one or two had fled to Germany, and a few others had been arrested, to be tried and sentenced as war criminals.

I did not know – nor did I ever discover – the identity of the informer who for unknown and unforgiveable reasons had reported father to the Gestapo, which resulted in father's internment and torture in the dreaded 'Little Fortress' of Terezin. I was determined not to think of the sadness of the past; what I needed more than anything was a little warmth and happiness in the rather bleak present. So on that Saturday night I fell asleep hugging Marta, remembering only the joyful moments of the day.

The next morning I met auntie at the station and together we called on the five people on mother's list. The warm friendliness I had encountered everywhere the previous day did not prepare me for the mixed reception we received. Two welcomed us with open arms, offering help and friendship, returning everything of their own accord, without even being asked. Two others parted with our possessions, or some of them, with great reluctance, not even trying to mask the resentment they felt at seeing us on their doorstep. Theirs was the look I was learning to expect and to dread, the look which almost shouted: 'Why did *my* Jew have to return?' The last call was on a woman who had been a close friend of mother's. She brazenly denied that she had ever been given anything of value to keep for us. I had been fond of her when I was a child and I could not bring myself to believe that she could be lying, and I convinced myself mother must have been confused. Then one day, months later, I saw that same woman in the street, wearing mother's fur coat. How bitterly disillusioned I felt then!

My aunt never believed the woman was telling the truth, and as we trudged back to the station, downcast and disappointed, her indignation knew no bounds. 'I never want to see Celakovice or any of those people again,' she vowed. 'How dare they call themselves your friends! And if you have any sense, my girl, you'll stay away too.'

I wanted to argue, to tell her that the town was full of genuine, friendly people, but I realised this was neither the time nor the place, and that in her present mood I would be wasting my breath.

Back in Prague, I could hardly bear to examine the few items, so precious to me, which were all that remained of our lovely home: father's favourite painting; a couple of rugs woven by mother; pillowcases and tablecloths she had embroidered; a few pieces from her large china collection which I always admired but was never allowed to touch; some of father's best-loved books, his watch and wedding ring; a sapphire and gold ring, pendant and earrings which father had given mother on the last birthday we had spent together (I knew that my parents had been ordered, as had all Jews, to hand over all their jewellery, silver and gold to the Germans, but according to my aunt, quite a lot had been hidden with friends). They had even bought two beautiful dinner services, one each for Eva and me – for our dowries. These were handed over to me complete. Of the furniture, only the grand piano and my sofa-bed remained. The piano was far too big for our little room, so we gave it to the local school, but we managed to squeeze the sofa-bed into the kitchen, so that Eva would have somewhere to sleep when she joined us in February.

The weekend left me feeling very confused. Disappointment and dejection alternated with elation; there were so many new impressions to absorb and come to terms with. Back at school, I confided in Seppi and Honza, who were also finding it hard to adjust.

Seppi, who originally came from Bratislava, was hit the hardest, for he had come back to not a soul. His parents had vanished, in fact his entire family had been exterminated. And now he was even separated from his younger brother Ernie who had been with him throughout the war years in Britain; Ernie was put into an orphanage, Seppie with a Prague family. He was unhappy there as in his new school, and eventually both he and his brother made their way back to the West.

At least Honza had a surviving uncle with whom he now made his home. Compared to Seppi, we were both extremely lucky . . .

Honza sympathised with me, for his experiences were similar to mine. He too had found several 'good friends' of his parents very reluctant to have anything to do with him, or to hand back his parents' possessions, while often mere acquaintances were very kind and caring. He told me about the old newsagent from whose shop his brother Franta used to buy a weekly magazine. When Honza met him by chance, the newsagent said, 'After they took Franta away, we were so sure he would return that we put by all the copies which have appeared since then. We kept them for him; please take them.' Franta was supposed to follow Honza to Britain in 1939, in the same transport in which my cousins should have been, but, like them, he never made it, and perished in the camps.

Shortly after my weekend in Celakovice, an attractive young woman appeared at our door. When she saw me, her face lit up and she threw her arms around me. 'Verusko, how you've grown!' she cried. I would have recognised that vibrant voice and those laughing eyes anywhere. It was Marenka, who used to help mother in the office, and sometimes even came on holiday with us to the mountains. Her happy bubbly personality made her a great favourite with all our family.

'I'm so sorry I missed you when you came to Celakovice,' she said, 'but I was away at the time. Marta told me you'd spent the night with her. Now, Janda and I have a nice big flat where you can have your own room whenever you want to come and stay. I've come to persuade Berta to share you with me. Your parents were always very good to me, and made me feel one of the family. This is my way of saying thank you to them, and besides, it will give me a chance to get to know this young "English" diamond all over again.'

I basked in Marenka's words. I had been her bridesmaid and I liked her enormously. I obstinately ignored all auntie's objections. After much persuading she agreed that I could spend some weekends with Marenka. Needless to say, I went the very next Saturday. That same night, after another day with Marta, when my happiness was tempered by bitter-sweet memories, Marenka came to tuck me in. Lying snuggly between the sheets, I said how pretty they were.

'Of course they're pretty,' Marenka nodded. 'Your mother chose them.' And she proceeded to tell me how this came about.

Apparently, Marenka's very strict mother didn't approve of Janda, with whom Marenka was in love, and tried her utmost to break up the romance; but my mother liked the young couple and often played Cupid. As well as providing them with opportunities to meet, she asked Marenka to help in the office far more often than was really necessary, and risked accusations of meanness, because instead of increasing her wages, all of which Marenka had to hand over to her mother, she secretly started buying linen for Marenka's 'bottom drawer'. Thanks to mother's excellent taste and unstinting generosity, by the time Janda walked his radiant

bride down the aisle with me in tow, she not only had a fine
dowry, but one provided by my mother!

The knowledge that the sheets which covered me had
been chosen and bought by mother, that she had touched
them, added extra warmth to my nights at Marenka's flat.
Mother's presence was everywhere: in the tablecloths,
towels, curtains, even the dishcloths! Marenka slipped into
my case many an article I particularly admired, so I could
share in the dowry my mother had bought her.

Such stories warmed and tormented me at the same time.
I wanted to be reminded of my childhood, to escape into it,
to keep my parents alive; and for that there was no better
place than my home town.

Though my aunt too had an open invitation, she was as
good as her word and never went to Celakovice again. In a
way, I wasn't sorry, but I felt guilty. I did need a rest from
her; she loved me dearly and denied me nothing, but life
with her was far from easy. She was now chronically
depressed and seemed unable to grasp any joy or comfort
which came her way. It was as if she had to do continual
penance for having survived. I was full of concern and
compassion, but it was difficult for me, a seventeen-year-
old, to live in such close confined proximity with a cheerless
person who lived almost as if waiting and wanting to die.

No wonder I found Marenka's happy nature a welcome
relief. She was so affectionate too, and not ashamed of
showing her feelings. A wistful, look, a sigh, or a long face
was all that was needed for her arms to fold around me and
hold me close, while her soothing, gentle voice lightened my
gloom. It was easy to respond to such warmth. Even the
congenial atmosphere of the flat helped me to relax. It was
bright and airy, usually filled with the tempting smell of
weekend baking, and echoed with music and laughter. Janda
had his own band, and one or two of the musicians were
always around. They were a jolly crowd, but then they were
unscarred by the war.

Some weeks after I started visiting Celakovice on a fairly
regular basis, Marenka took me aside. 'I have a letter,' she
said, 'It was written to you and Eva by your mother before

she was taken to Terezin. I waited until I felt you were
strong and adjusted enough to read it. Be brave, for her
sake, and don't get too upset.'

Alone in my room I opened the envelope. The crisp white
paper looked brand new, and the words so clear, as if the
letter had been written only yesterday . . .

1 January 1943

My dearest children,

My life belonged to you, and you and your dear father were the
happiness of my life. If only this letter were not to say goodbye,
if only fate, which has treated me so cruelly, would once more
allow me to be reunited with you and the one we all so dearly love,
if only we could resume our life together, life filled with joy and
love . . .

When I was sixteen years old I met your father. Never did I
think that one person could give so much love and happiness. My
life turned into the most joyful dream, the most wonderful fairy tale.
When we were married on 12 December 1920, I was the happiest
person alive. Four perfect years went by and then you arrived,
Evicko, who are nineteen years old today, to whom I should like to
say so many beautiful things, but to whom – and to my dear
Veruska – I am now writing this sad letter, yet hoping that one day
I may be able to tell you everything, to hold you close to my
anguished heart.

On 13 November, two days after your father's birthday, I was
numbed by the cruel blow which fate dealt me – and you – my
dearest children, on that day . . .

They took away father, your good, kind father who took such
good care of us, whose only wish was your happiness, who so
hoped to be reunited with you one day, who so looked forward to
that day; he lived for you, he had faith in you, and he believed – so
very very much . . .

For six weeks he was kept at the county court in Boleslav, where
the Gestapo had taken him, then he was transferred to the Little
Fortress in Terezin.

On the 12th of this month it will be my turn to leave. Since the
beginning of the month I have been sharing my home with the
Goldsmidt boys from next door. Their father is in the same prison
as yours; their mother died a year ago, and so I shall now go with

them. I am not afraid of going, for I shall meet your grandfather again, and auntie Berta, Mila and Karel; the others have gone on to Poland. I fear nothing, but I am filled with anxiety and endless pain. Your father and I wanted to live, work and suffer together, and now they have torn us apart. I promise you, my dear children, that I shall be brave, that the thought of you and of our dearest one will be my strength and that I shall not give up – but will fate allow me to see happier days? . . .

This letter will be given to you; always hold these friends in high esteem and never forget their goodness.

And now, my dear children, on behalf of your father and myself, I wish you – not only for the new year, not only for Eva's birthday, but for the rest of your life . . . Be happy, be brave. We gave you love, we gave you the foundations of life, we wanted to give you more, so much more . . . How I wish that fate would make up to you all it has refused us, how I hope that your life will flow smoothly, filled with joy and happiness. Remember your home and us, but do not grieve. Your whole life lies before you, life which you will build at the side of your husbands. I give my blessings to them and to your children; I shall be watching over you from Heaven, and praying for your happiness.

I embrace you and I bless you,

Your *maminka*

The words swam before my eyes. What they had had to face – and each of them alone – and that was only the beginning . . .

Until I read mother's letter, my parents' suffering was something shadowy, undefined. Now reality hit me with full force and I was beginning to see with shattering clarity the mental and physical torment they must have endured.

For weeks afterwards I went about in a sort of trance, leading what might pass for a normal life, yet hardly aware of the outside world. Eventually I sought comfort in my diary which, since my return, had lain neglected and unused, for the incentive to write had gone. My diaries had been kept for them, only for them . . . But now I had to pour out my anguish and talk to mother.

22 December 1945

My dearest *maminko,*

I have read your beautiful letter so many times and can find no words to describe how I feel each time. I dare not read it too often, for whenever I do my only wish is to die, to be with you and father. It is the most beautiful, the most noble letter ever written. Your deep love and utter devotion to us and to father flows from every word, as does your unselfishness, your courage and determination. Oh, how my heart goes out to you as I see you, devastated by pain and the cruelty of fate, bravely writing these lines, yet still hoping, still believing. I see you so clearly, you seem so real, yet you are a vision which always disappears. I feel and see you always and everywhere, my heart weeps and aches for you, I yearn to embrace you, to cover your dear face with kisses, to be with you, only you . . .

Why did God take you away from us? Why?

The grief I suffered in England after hearing of your death cannot be compared with the pain I feel now. There, I was accustomed to a life without you and father, but here everything reminds me of you both, of our dashed hopes and lost happiness. And whatever I have forgotten of my childhood, Auntie Berta and our family friends are always ready to fill in for me. I would never tire of listening to them if they talked day after day, from morning until night. It soothes, in a painful sort of way, and each time I learn a little more about you, I feel a little closer to you. How everyone loved you! I am so proud to be the daughter of such parents.

I had to write today, and I feel better for having done so. Until now I didn't have the strength to take a pen and describe my feelings in this diary which in the past had shared everything that happened to me, my every thought – but then I kept it for you. Today I felt so forlorn, so desperately unhappy, I could not bear my inner loneliness. I feel a little less despondent now.

I promise, my dearest *maminko,* that I shall try not to be sad at Christmas. I shall think of you and father, and of

Eva too, and when I light the candles on the tree I shall look up into the sky and imagine that you are both gazing down upon me and auntie through the window.

Once I had begun to come to terms with what I had learned from mother's letter, I was consumed with the need to know more about my parents' fate. It would be harrowing, but I realised that the more I knew, the closer to them I would feel.

I tackled Auntie Berta, Mila and Karel. Although still reluctant to talk, they eventually added some substance to the vague outlines of my knowledge.

Some weeks after father's arrest and imprisonment in the Little Fortress of Terezin, mother, then still at home, received a smuggled note asking her to hand over a large sum of money to a certain Nazi officer. Mother carried out the instructions without knowing the purpose of this bribe – just praying fervently it would help father in some way – hardly daring to hope that it could secure his release.

I could imagine her immense joy and relief when, shortly after writing the letter to Eva and me, she suddenly saw his tall figure in the crowded hall in Terezin into which thousands of newly arrived Jews had been herded. She had arrived there, exhausted, bewildered and distressed after a long journey in a sealed cattle truck crammed with the remaining Jews from our area. Crying our father's name she battled her way to his side and fell into his arms. The weeks of torture had turned his black hair snow-white; there was not an ounce of flesh on his body, his finger and toenails had been ripped out – but he was alive. The bribe had served its purpose and father had been transferred from the Little Fortress to the Terezin ghetto. To my parents this must have seemed a miraculous release; yet, sadly, his life had not been saved, only prolonged, as was his suffering.

Women and men were kept apart in overcrowded freezing living-quarters, but at that stage father and mother could still meet and talk almost daily. Father never recovered his strength. He had always been a heavy smoker, and even here he was willing to barter his meagre rations for cigarettes.

Mother never saw grandfather again; by the time she arrived at Terezin, he had died. This proud, refined man was confined to his hard cold bunk in barracks – 'the men's hospital for the elderly'. Stripped of his dignity, he almost lost his reason, so great was his bewilderment and despair. But then many internees, particularly the old, lost their sanity in Terezin . . .

Perhaps this was why mother and Auntie Berta, who were now reunited, volunteered to nurse the mentally ill. It was gruelling and distressing work, in atrocious conditions, which was why most prisoners were reluctant to take on such duties. Mother and my aunt hoped that this in itself would save them from selection for deportation to Poland. Their hopes were short-lived: Auntie Berta, Mila and Karel were the first to leave for Auschwitz; then came father's turn, and mother was alone once more. She followed them in January 1944 and was placed in camp B-IIb, housed in large dilapidated stables – rotting relics from the First World War – five hundred prisoners to a stable. Miraculously, here she found Auntie Berta and Mila again, and was told that father and Karel were in the same camp, but all contact between male and female prisoners was now forbidden.

During the hard winter of 1944 the mortality rate soared. With only coffee substitute for breakfast, beet soup for lunch, and a slice of black bread, often 'enriched' with ground glass, for supper, many died of starvation or from the bitter cold. Sickness and disease took their toll, as did the hard labour. Men and women alike had to carry huge boulders on their backs, to what purpose no one knew. Yet these were the lucky ones, because the majority of the prisoners from Terezin were marched straight into the gas chambers – the two young boys who had lived next door to us in Celakovice among them.

In June 1944 came the order to liquidate camp B-IIb. 'Doctor' Mengele, the notorious Nazi murderer, was in command of this operation. From the ten thousand prisoners who had to parade naked before him he selected two thousand men and a thousand women, all capable of work, to go elsewhere. The remaining seven thousand, which included all children under the age of sixteen, were taken to the gas chambers. Father and Karel, who had, until then, faced their nightmarish existence together, were now split up: Karel was sent with one group to the Schwarzheide concentration camp; father was in the second group which went to the Bleckhammer camp in Silesia. The conditions in both camps were so appalling that only a handful of men survived. Father was not one of them. A surviving fellow-prisoner later told us that he could almost swear that he had seen father shot during one of the regular death marches in December 1944 . . .

Mother, Auntie Berta and Mila went on to the concentration camp in Hamburg where the women worked as labourers, shovelling away the rubble of bombed houses. They had to work even through heavy air-raids, and many of the prisoners were killed by Allied bombs.

At first mother was spared this dangerous, back-breaking work, for her excellent culinary capabilities earned her a place in the officers' kitchen. More importantly, this provided her with the opportunity to steal a little extra food to supplement the prisoners' terrible diet. Both Mila and Berta, with whom she shared her 'spoils', swear that this saved their lives.

Later, mother was ousted from her job by a younger, prettier Jewess, but she did not have to endure hard labour for long. On 23 or 24 March 1945, those who were still alive were taken to Bergen-Belsen where there was no food or medicine, and there left to die. By the time the British Army liberated the camp on 15 April, starvation, typhus and other diseases had claimed many of the survivors; thousands died later. Mother, Tommy and Honza – our cousins – were among them . . .

Every detail hit me like a physical blow. Even then I could not absorb the full horror. No one could. I found no comfort in the knowledge that mother at least had lived to see peace. It was a bitter irony that she died, having suffered so much, after being freed, without even seeing us, when she had so much to live for . . .

'I should have been with her,' I sobbed, but Auntie Berta turned on me, almost accusingly, and cried: 'Don't ever think or say that again! Knowing that you and Eva were safe was the only happiness she had. Had you been with her, her suffering would have been a thousand times greater.

'Can you imagine the pain it would have caused her – even while she was in Terezin – to see you living in children's quarters, pale, hungry and frightened? Waking up each morning wondering whether this would be the day when you, her child, would be selected to die – or be reprieved for a while longer? Can you imagine the anguish she would have felt seeing the sad questioning look in your eyes, the look of every child in the ghetto, silently asking: "Why do we have to live in this dark grey place? Why can't we go home? Why are we being punished?"

'The only crime those children had committed was to be born a Jew. And for that sin most of them perished.' (More than 15,000 children passed through Terezin; a hundred survived.) 'Your safety was your parents' only comfort, only joy, and they thanked God every night for that blessing. Remember that – always.'

I looked at my aunt with compassion and respect. 'And I thank God that you were with mother and that she didn't have to face each day alone,' I whispered. 'That was another great blessing.'

'If only she had survived,' Auntie Berta sighed, 'how different our lives would be.'

She misses her as much as I do, I thought, and my heart went out to her. From then on I tried all the harder to brighten her days and make her believe that life was still worth living. At times I succeeded, and when on the rare occasions she relaxed and a flicker of a smile crossed her face, I felt richly rewarded.

There was something else I felt compelled to do. Though father had had me baptised, I was born a Jew, and my parents had perished because they were Jews. I owed it to them and to myself to return to our faith. In this way I would

They fell so the nation could live

In Prague's Jewish Museum, all that remains of 15,000 children are a few crayon drawings on scraps of paper . . .

. . . But my children could play happily with Auntie Berta on a Suffolk beach

June 1985: the best-represented class of the reunion. From left to right:
Harry, Honza, Helena, Bobby, Hedy, Eva, Olga, myself; Seppi and Peter at the front

In the past we sang for the local inhabitants; now the children of Llanwrtyd Wells sang for us

Bryn Jones, the mayor, being presented with the chain of office

How we feel about this little town is stated plainly
on the plaque placed in the grounds of our old school

LLANWRTYD WELLS. THE SMALLEST TOWN IN THE LAND.
REMAINS FOREVER THE GREATEST IN OUR HEARTS.

This lime was planted by the old boys and girls
of the Czechoslovak Secondary School (Abernant 1943-45),
now scattered throughout the world.

With Eva, still the best sister in the world

My 'little English mummy' on her 91st birthday

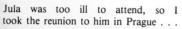

Jula was too ill to attend, so I took the reunion to him in Prague . . .

. . . And couldn't miss visiting Celakovice and Marta at the same time.

honour their memory. And I swore I would never be ashamed, but proud of being a Jew.

By the time Eva joined us in February 1946, our roles had almost reversed. She had nourished my spirit during the years when a shared future with our parents was what we lived for, and our main reason for wanting to return. Feeling tougher and wiser, and far less idealistic than when I had arrived, I warned Eva in my letters not to expect too much, that in some ways she would be disillusioned and that at times she might feel more a foreigner in her own country than she had felt as a refugee in Britain. I found her unsure of herself, and a little apprehensive, and was not surprised when after some months she decided to return to England. Accustomed as she now was to the British way of life, she found the rigours of post-war Czechoslovakia too difficult to take, especially without our parents.

She asked me to leave too, but much as I hated the thought of another parting, I decided, after some hesitation, to stay. There was always the possibility that I would follow later, but for the moment I wanted to concentrate on my studies and to make the most of all the things I loved about my country.

I was also leading a busy social life, and had a string of admirers. I was constantly changing boyfriends and falling in and out of love, and more often than not I was in love with several boys at the same time. I needed to be loved and to love in return – to take what life offered when it had robbed me of so much. I was enthusiastic about each new relationship, but every suitor eventually fell short of the high standards I set him: subconsciously I was searching for a person worthy of the pure tender love I had saved for my parents, and such a paragon simply did not exist.

Inevitably, some of my boyfriends came from Celakovice. I spent most of my free time there, it was my favourite place. But, much as I loved it, I knew right from the start I could never settle there, not only because I would be haunted by the shadows of the past, but also because I had outgrown the

simple narrow life of a small town. I felt genuine affection
for many of the local people but I had little in common with
them. For the time being, Celakovice was a very necessary,
bright haven to which I escaped whenever my conscience
and my aunt allowed me, a haven in which I could share in
the happy simplicity and normality of my friends' lives.

One of the rare entries in my diary describes my first
romance at home:

16 April 1946

It was so beautiful – my first love in Czechoslovakia. It
crept up on me gently, step by step: first there was
interest, then friendship and attraction, until suddenly
love loomed so large that I lived, more or less, for
Saturdays and Sundays spent with you, Jirka. During the
week I lived on memories, counting the days, the hours to
the next weekend . . .

How well I remember our first meeting! Marenka took
me to my first dance in Celakovice; Janda's band was
playing, of course. Only a handful of people recognised
me then. Franta was there, and he kept asking me to
dance, telling me how bored he had been until I sailed into
Celakovice like a ray of sunshine. He said he fell in
love with me at first sight. Then you asked me to dance,
and I so enjoyed dancing with you and talking to you. We
liked each other the moment we met. You were so formal,
and called me 'Miss'. You came at a time when my heart
was still heavy with sadness and pain, when I longed for
new friends to help me forget, help me take up my new
life. You and Franta seemed like an answer to a prayer.

Franta mentioned that he had to go to Prague on
Sunday night, so we arranged to travel by train together.
At first he sat quietly beside me, but as we neared Prague,
he suddenly grabbed my hand. I knew I should pull it
away, I knew I shouldn't raise his hopes, yet I let my hand
rest in his, and felt strangely comforted.

Franta, of course, had nothing to do in Prague, and he
caught the very next train back . . . Before he left, we
arranged to meet the following Saturday night in

Celakovice. All would have been well if you hadn't turned up.

I can see it all as if it were yesterday. After a quick hello to Marenka, I ran to see Marta, but on the way I bumped into you. When you asked me to come for a walk, I promptly forgot all about Marta. It was a lovely hot day, we were relaxed and happy, we laughed and joked and you stopped calling me 'Miss'. Goodness knows what got into me, but I asked you to come along on my date with Franta. I thought to myself, 'Marta will come too, and we'll have a good time.' But Marta had other ideas. 'You stick to your boyfriends,' she said, 'and I'll stick to mine.' My pleas and protests fell on deaf ears.

That evening I found myself in a most embarrassing situation. Both of you were waiting for me on the corner, eyeing each other warily. It was terrible. Neither of you said a word, so I took out a bar of chocolate and broke it in half, but I didn't know which one of you to give the first piece to! We walked to the woods where some scouts were singing round a bonfire. We watched for a while, and suddenly both of you, one on each side of me, took hold of my hand. I nearly died, I just didn't know which one to let go. Eventually I wriggled out of Franta's hold . . .

On the way home Franta looked so dejected that I felt sorry for him, but not enough to stop you, Jirka, from linking your arm with mine. By the time I went to bed, I was in an awful mood. Instead of finding two new friends, as I had hoped, I realised that I would have to choose between you, and the thought haunted me even in my sleep.

Next day you were waiting for me, and we went back to the woods. I was very grumpy, mainly because I was ashamed of treating Franta so badly and causing him pain. I just couldn't understand myself at all.

In the woods we stretched out on the mossy carpet, gazed into the thick crowns of the trees and listened to the song of birds. Then you spoilt it when you leaned over and tried to kiss me. I was so startled I jumped to my feet, told you off, and stalked away home. I was so furious, I didn't even say goodbye.

When I told Marta what had happened, she said: 'I
didn't want to run Jirka down, but he is rather forward,
and a dreadful flirt.'

Determined to make amends, I sent Franta a letter of
apology, and a letter to you, saying that I never wanted to
go out with you again. But when we met three weeks later
at another dance, my heart missed a beat. You asked me
to meet you in Prague, and to your astonishment, and
mine, I agreed; so it all started again.

I so loved the mushroom season! We always went in a
foursome: Marta and Vlada, you and I. What fun we had!
Getting up at dawn, coming home ravenous to tuck into
our freshly picked mushrooms and eggs. It was on the way
to the woods that I first let you kiss me, and you were so
pleased that I didn't fly off the handle again. Then came
the winter, and football matches, skating, and dancing
every Saturday. On New Year's Eve we danced the night
away, and at midnight you gave me the first kiss of the
year. We were seen, but who cares? I knew you pretty
well by then, and though I hadn't forgotten Marta's
warning, I pushed the word 'flirt' out of my mind.

I don't think that you took anyone else out during the
six months we went out with each other, but somehow a
gulf opened between us, and grew wider and wider. We
bridged it several times, but it always reappeared.
Eventually I suggested that we stop seeing each other; you
looked hurt, but it wasn't long before you started going
around with other girls. Marta was right, you are just a
flirt. I should have listened to her in the first place. But
you did love me! I know you did! But now that I know the
real you, I wouldn't want to go out with you again. Since
we stopped seeing each other, two months ago, you've
already had three new girlfriends. You're great, but
you're a flirt, a terrible flirt . . .

It had to end sometime.

I was so absorbed trying to establish my new life and identity
that I saw very little of my friends from the Czech school in
Wales, particularly during the first two years. When Honza

organised a small get-together in Prague, I discovered that
we were all in a similar situation, and finding the going
tough. The majority still felt, to some extent, like lost sheep.
We shared wistful memories of our days at school when we
were still hopeful. How young and naïve we'd been, we
thought as we looked back. We failed to realise the strength
of the bond forged amidst the Welsh hills.

The pleasure of meeting old friends compensated to some
extent for the coolness and occasional animosity I was still
meeting at my new school in Prague. In winter 1947 I
opened my diary again, and indignantly wrote:

Today I lost the last remnants of my faith in mankind.
Until I returned to Czechoslovakia, I was an out and out
idealist, but I am sad to say that my short time here has
cured me of my idealism. It was the school, 'the faithful
governess of youth', which finally snapped the slender
remaining threads of my conviction that the world is not
such a bad place and that people, on the whole, are kind.

I've often been told that schooldays are the happiest
days of one's life, and that school is there to instruct, to
show the right path to follow, the right goals to strive for.
Oh yes, when I think of my school in Britain, then I know
the saying can be true! I am convinced that the time I
spent there was one of the loveliest chapters of my life.
That was a school where everyone helped and respected
everyone else, a school which I remember with a smile
and an ache in my heart that those days will never
return . . .

Yet it was my school in Prague which finally crushed my
faith in righteousness. Why am I so often singled out and
victimised by some of the teachers? Why do I get low
marks even when I know I've done well? Once, when I
summoned up courage and asked why, the only answer
was a curt 'Because I felt like it!' That one short
incomprehensible sentence froze any further objections
on my tongue. Today I was unfairly treated again by a
master whom I always respected and in whom I had faith,
and that hurt even more. One more disappointment, one

more example of how hard it is to find truth and justice here . . .

It was a relief when in summer 1947 I left the school and enrolled at Charles University in Prague. By then the political scene was rapidly changing and I was beginning to find being pro-British more of a stigma than being a Jew. But I kept well out of politics. I just wanted to be left in peace to get on with my life.

I deluded myself that I had settled down, that I could be happy – until the day, in Celakovice, when my current boyfriend turned to me and said, almost jokingly: 'Have you heard my new nickname?' And when I shook my head, he replied: 'Jew-lover'.

Even my beloved home town never seemed quite the same after that . . .

Some time later, I went on a boat trip with Jula whom I had seen only once since our days in Wales. The captain of the paddle-steamer was jovial and chatty. For some reason, he singled us out, produced a bottle of wine and invited us to share it with him. Soon he was lost in reminiscences of the war and occupation. 'Those lousy Germans,' he growled. 'The only favour they did us was to kill so many Jews. It's a shame they didn't do the job properly and finish off all those bastards. You know the saying: "The best Jew is a dead Jew,"' and he laughed derisively.

We did not laugh with him. I stood, rooted to the spot, and looked at Jula. His eyes mirrored my own deep hurt. He squeezed my hand, wordlessly urging me to stay silent. I choked back the words of protest which rose in my throat and turned my back on the captain who was still laughing at his 'joke'.

It was then that I made up my mind. Eva had been bombarding me with letters, asking me to join her. I would go to England. I knew anti-semitism existed there too, as it existed and still exists everywhere, but surely anywhere in the world it would be easier to bear than in my own – still beloved – country.

Although my decision was made, I hated the thought of

leaving, and particularly parting from Auntie Berta. I dreaded telling her, but she made it easy for me: she not only understood, she encouraged me to go.

'Have you forgotten that it was I who begged you to stay in England in the first place?' she reminded me. 'I was certain that life would be better and easier for you there than here. Now you have proved that I was right. Never mind, you obviously had to find out for yourself. Don't worry about me. I've had my life, but yours lies ahead of you. And who knows, perhaps I'll join you and Eva one day.'

I was also sad to leave Richard, my current boyfriend. An ardent mountaineer, he was strong and silent, a man of moods, like the mountains themselves. He taught me to climb, and had done his utmost to teach me to follow my head and not my heart. His ruthless logic helped me to stand by my decision. But saying goodbye to him and to my aunt was an awful wrench:

30 January 1949

When I think of those last days in Prague, how swiftly they passed – far too swiftly. Soon it was my last evening . . .

Mila and Karel came and went, then at midnight Auntie Berta went to bed. Richard and I went on sitting in the kitchen by the open stove, with a half-empty bottle of cherry brandy and a couple of sandwiches. The hours ticked away, so mercilessly fast, cutting shorter and shorter those last moments of happiness when I was in his arms, cursing absurd reality which in a few hours would carry me away from him, perhaps for ever. But the hands of the clock, which I watched so anxiously, moved on and on in relentless silence.

Then came morning, and the station, where other friends waited to say goodbye. The dreaded whistle blew, and I saw only Richard, strong and unbending as ever, with his eyes saying it all. What we said to each other with our eyes then could never be put into words. Mine spoke of despair, hope, love and commitment, whilst his implored me to be strong, to let reason prevail. And there was something else deep in his eyes, something which, until then, had been hidden and unsaid: I saw love there, and it warmed, yet grieved, my heart.

As the train left, and he stood there, apart from the others, waving his hat, I wanted to laugh and to shout that this couldn't really be happening.

But it was happening . . .

Auntie Berta rode with me on that bleak January morning all the way to the frontier. She sat by my side and held my hand, and gave me strength as she always did when I needed her, and I wished we had the carriage to ourselves so I could, without shame, hide my face in her lap and cry my heart out.

On the border I had to part from her too. I can see her now as she stood by the barrier, a forlorn slight figure alone in the wintry gloom, her waving arm barely visible through the thick flurry of snow which had already obscured her dark winter coat, her hat and her tears.

I was filled with an overpowering sense of sadness at leaving her, and my home and country, for the second time . . .

9

British by Choice

IT WAS GOOD to be back in Britain which was, after all, my second home. I felt more of a native than a foreigner here. Any doubts I may have had were soon dispelled by the welcome I received from the Rainfords and all my old English friends. It almost seemed as if I had never been away.

What pleased me most was to be with Eva again. Our deep affection for each other which had grown so much through the war years had hardly had a chance to surface during Eva's brief stay in Prague. But now, secure in the knowledge that we both intended to settle in England, we turned to each other again for support and understanding and rediscovered our sisterly love. Eva would have liked to go on mothering me as she had done in wartime, but I gently pointed out that at the age of twenty I must stand on my own feet and make my own way in life. The first step was to close the door firmly on the past and to concentrate on putting down roots for the future.

I had failed to find happiness in my country. Perhaps I had expected too much, perhaps I had not been willing to give enough of myself. Whatever the reason, this time I was determined not to fail, but to become fully integrated into the British way of life.

Towards the end of that first year I married Michael, a handsome, charming, non-Jewish Englishman. We were in love, but we had very little in common, and in character and background were poles apart. Yet we remained together for more than thirty years during which we raised a family of three; I think it is to our credit that though the marriage has foundered, our respect for one another and a fond friendship have survived.

My marriage is not the subject of this book; it is enough to say that I have no regrets and that I feel deep gratitude to God for allowing me to watch my children grow up in the security of their home and their parents' love, without them ever having to face the wrench of parting, and the horrors and the tragedy of war and the holocaust. In this way God has made up to me for the anguish, and for the great void my own parents' death left in my young life.

Eva married a Welsh doctor and had a family, and we saw a good deal of each other until, much to my regret, they emigrated to New Zealand, and we were separated again. I missed her terribly, and I miss her still, though we write frequently and see each other when we can.

Auntie Berta paid us a long visit each year, and though my family adored her, she decided she was too old and too set in her ways to move to a foreign country. Until she died in 1981 she remained a very special, very dear part of my life, and she heartily approved of my new role – that of a typical British housewife. My performance was so convincing that I even fooled myself that this was all I wanted, all I needed in life. So anxious was I to be at one with my adopted nation, that far from forcing my own background and beliefs on my children, I tried to forget that I was Czech – I almost tried to forget that I was Jewish – but it was all a pretence . . .

I did not visit Prague again until the spring of 1968. By that time the trauma of long-distance travel had become too much for my aunt and she suggested that I come to her instead. After an absence of twenty years I found it was a very emotional homecoming. With each passing day I felt more vulnerable, less sure of myself, my old resolves crumbling away. Then one day Jula, a great connoisseur of Prague, took time off to reintroduce me to the city we both loved. In the afternoon we wandered into the Jewish quarter and visited the old synagogue and the cemetery where ancient tombstones, weathered by centuries, rise from the graves at eerie irregular angles, while the shrill haunting cries of the many black ravens which live in the tall poplar trees above fill the cemetery with a ghostly lament for the dead.

Thoughtful and subdued, we left the cemetery and entered the adjoining museum. We found ourselves in a small room. The walls were whitewashed and bare, except for drawings, some on scraps of paper, in crayon or pencil, and a sign which read: 'This is all that remains of the 15,000 Jewish children who passed through Terezin.'

I looked at the drawings, some of which depicted the cruel reality of the children's everyday lives: the barracks, the stretchers, the transports, the funerals and executions . . . and then I turned to other drawings evoking their lost happy childhood: toys, plates heaped with food, meadows bright with flowers, colourful birds and butterflies which those innocent children were doomed never to see again. And in those drawings I saw mother and father, my own cousins and young friends, and all the thousands upon thousands who died – and suddenly I saw myself: this is all that would have remained of me had my mother and father not had the foresight and courage to send me to England . . .

All at once I could not bear to look any longer, nor to stay in that little room filled with tourists, and I fled up a narrow, winding staircase, ignoring a notice which said 'No entry'. There, at the top of the stairs, stood Jula, the tears running down his cheeks as they were down mine, and we clung to each other and cried together as the two Czech Jewish children we had been, who had lost so much and who were so lost themselves. This was the first and only time I let another human being enter the shrine I carried in my heart for my parents.

This was a turning point in my life, because it was there, in that small museum of the holocaust, that my search for my identity ended. I realised at long last that by shutting out the past I had closed the door on my inner self – that I would never find peace and true happiness unless I accepted myself for what I was: Jewish by race, Czech by birth, and British by choice.

Year followed year, and my life was richer and fuller now that it included regular visits to Prague. I no longer criticised, nor chased lost illusions, but accepted the country for what it was, the good and the bad. Whenever I was there, Celakovice still drew me like a magnet. The town had mushroomed, and now wore an air of cleanliness and prosperity. Only our old house still looked shabby and sad as if mourning the bygone days when it was the loving home of my family. Marta and I still liked to wander hand in hand down memory lane to the river bank and to the woods where we played as children, and later went courting, or to look in at the gym-cum-cinema-cum-ballroom where, chaperoned by Marenka, we often danced as teenagers to the strains of Janda's band.

I also found myself increasingly drawn to the friends I had made at the Czech school in Wales. I had never lost touch with my closest friends, whether they had remained in Czechoslovakia, or settled in Britain, or elsewhere. Although through the years we had drifted apart, the realisation was slowly dawning on me that we were closer to each other than to almost anyone else. We had shared our most impressionable years and were victims of a similar fate, which helped our relationship to survive distance and time.

By the time Seppi, Honza, Harry and I met in London in the summer of 1984 for the dinner during which the idea of the reunion was born and planned, I was sharing my life with Harry, with whom I had shared a classroom more than forty years before. Seppi and Honza had both left Czechoslovakia after I had, Seppi to build a brilliant career in journalism in Canada and America, while Honza, like me, had settled in England. Harry never returned to Czechoslovakia but remained in Britain with his sister and parents. He too has one marriage behind him, and we both appreciate our second chance of happiness.

Judging by my own experiences, I was fully confident, though the other three were a little doubtful, that the idea of the reunion would be well received and the event a success, yet even I was astonished at the overwhelming response. It seemed that nearly everyone we managed to trace in all corners of the globe during the ensuing months of detective work, was harbouring a secret desire to return to the little haven where he or she had spent their schooldays during the war and to meet old friends. Naturally, there were a few who did not wish to be involved and others we were unable to trace. Sadly, we found that death had claimed several pupils and members of staff, and old age and illness stopped many from attending.

When I was trying to locate Miss Mackenzie, who had been not only a teacher but also a generous, warm-hearted friend to most of us, I felt rather guilty that I had been so absorbed in my own life that I had lost contact with her. When I finally found Miss Mac, I reproached myself all the more, because she was suffering from a terminal illness. Almost too late, I showered her with letters of encouragement and support, and gave her all the news. Although her own life was nearly over, she was with us in spirit at the reunion, for when we arrived at the Abernant Lake Hotel there was a message of love and good wishes waiting for us. She passed away three days later. I console myself with the thought that we had at least brightened her last days on this earth and that she died knowing she was remembered. Yet I cannot but ask myself, as I have done many times already: why did we not think of organising the reunion ten years earlier, when our numbers were not so depleted, when old age and illness had not yet knocked on so many of our doors?

I was grieved to learn from Jula that our invitation to the reunion coincided with an unfavourable report from his doctors, and a very firm invitation for a hospital stay which he had to accept. His presence was sorely missed by everyone, but particularly by me.

All my other close friends managed to come. Alice, recently widowed, travelled from Prague; Margit flew in from Holland, and Olga from New York. In all, over seventy old pupils, some with wives or husbands, and a few members of the staff came together for one brilliantly sunny June weekend which, from start to finish, had an extraordinary dreamlike quality.

It was a weekend which took us back in time. A weekend when everyone forgot their social status, achievements and failures, and we were all equal. Many of the poor refugee boys and girls, some orphaned by the war, fuelled perhaps by adversity, had worked their way up to the top of their various professions: there were members of the diplomatic service, members of Parliament, and United Nations delegates, doctors and dentists, even a couple of millionaires, and a real Lady . . .

In spite of tremendously varied personal circumstances and experiences, in spite of being scattered across continents for the past four decades, there is still an indefinable bond which makes us 'a family' – a special and unique group of brothers and sisters. We were all greatly moved to discover that this bond still exists and still holds and that our friendship, understanding, common trust and willingness to help would always be there. To my mind, this merely underlines the truth of the well-worn saying that good can come out of evil. Besides, would any of us have had the drive and determination to succeed in life had we not been so cruelly affected by world events?

As I sat back at the end of the last meal of the weekend, watching the animated faces which only two days ago I had barely recognised, but which were now familiar and dear to me, I felt honoured and proud that I had played a small part in bringing us all together.

We planted the national tree of Czechoslovakia, the lime, in the hotel grounds to mark the occasion. Many of the town folk joined us for the ceremony, bringing with them the junior school choir. As if to thank us for the concerts we, as children, had given the village, they sang for us now, dressed in their national costume.

While we listened and watched, remembering our happy years, we thought of our old friend, Jim Jones, and how he would have loved to be part of the reunion. Sadly, this man who had loomed so large in our adolescence, had died, and been laid to rest in an unmarked grave. His corner shop had been demolished years ago, and on the site, right in the heart of the town, a small green now overlooks the river Irfon. It was there that we decided to place a commemorative seat, dedicated to all the people of Llanwrtyd Wells. Somehow I think it will be known as 'Jim's seat' and that it will be a more fitting memorial than a gravestone.

Such was the friendship shown to us during our stay by the local inhabitants that we wanted to show our gratitude for their past and present kindness in a practical way. When a former pupil offered a substantial contribution to our fund, we agreed to present the town with a Mayoral Chain of Office. In this way we would have a permanent place in the town's history, just as Llanwrtyd Wells has a permanent place in our hearts and lives.

When the coach was about to leave for London and all the goodbyes had been said, a group of our Welsh friends, led by the Mayor, lined the lane and burst into song. We drove off with tears in our eyes, the words of 'Come home again to Wales' ringing in our ears. We knew that now contacts had been renewed, old friendships reaffirmed and new ones made, we would be back, singly or in groups, again and again. For, as the inscription on the plaque by the lime tree reads:

> Llanwrtyd Wells, the smallest town in the land,
> remains for ever the greatest in our hearts.

I felt both sadness and contentment as the coach sped away. Our journey marked the end of an unforgettable weekend which can probably never be repeated, yet somehow I knew that in a way the reunion would go on for ever – that this was yet another beginning . . .

The emotions and memories stirred and rekindled during those three memorable days gave me the strength, in fact almost compelled me to tell my story. My task is completed; I seem to have travelled a full circle, reopening doors I had left locked for most of my life, reliving moments of beauty and happiness, sadness and pain. Once again, I became the little girl who cried real pearls, the fiercely patriotic homesick refugee, the hopeful, then devastated teenager, the disillusioned young woman.

The shrine for my parents still lies deep in my heart, where my love for them burns, undiminished by time. And when I feel unhappy, lost or lonely, and cry out, 'Where is my home?' – it is to this shrine that I turn as I have done ever since I went back to my roots in 1968 and found my identity. It was then that I discovered that my home was deep inside me, a precious and private refuge. Home is love, and you, my dearest ones, are still home to me . . .